372.21　　　　　　　cop. 1
Sku
SKUTCH
To start a school

DATE DUE		
~~MAY 2 1982~~		
~~JAN 18 '90~~		

TO START A SCHOOL

TO START A SCHOOL

Margaret Skutch and Wilfrid G. Hamlin

with photographs by George S. Zimbel

Little, Brown and Company – Boston -Toronto

Library of Congress Catalog Card No. 76–170165

First Edition

T01/72

Illustrations by George S. Zimbel
for Educational Facilities Laboratories

Published simultaneously in Canada by Little, Brown & Company
(Canada) Limited
Printed in the United States of America

Preface

Seven years ago I started a school. I started it with no experience, a little training, and practically no capital — but with a lot of energy and a very firm conviction that I wanted to make just as good an environment for learning as it was possible to make. Today the Early Learning Center in Stamford, Connecticut, is visited by teachers and parents from all over the country, and thousands of people have seen the film about it which was made under the sponsorship of the Educational Facilities Laboratory. Those seven years have been the busiest and most important years in my life. This book is about them: about the school as it is today and about how it came to be. It's about architecture and equipment, parents, money, what teachers say and do. Most of all it's about children and how they learn.

My friend Will Hamlin and I wrote the book for two main reasons: First, what goes on at the Early Learning Center is an illustration of ideas about education interesting to a growing number of Americans. They are the ideas of that turn-of-the-century genius and social reformer Maria Montessori, and of those inspired educators of a half century later who developed free schools in the English county of Leicestershire. Basically, they are ideas about how children teach themselves and each other when their great curiosity about the world is matched by materials and equipment through which it can be satisfied, nourished, extended. We believe they are important ideas, useful as a basis for any thinking about education, with people of all ages.

One reason we think they're important ideas is that they're based on a view of learning as a human activity, not a mechanical one. At our school we know children as individuals wonderfully different from each other. Sometimes we generalize about two-year-olds or six-year-olds, but it's only a generalization, and Liza, whose third birthday was celebrated this fall, is first and last Liza, a single and separate human being with all the complexities, potentials, and problems that being human entails. Liza's way of learning, her particular curiosity about sounds, the way she greets her mother at noon: these are all part of her life in the school. And it is to that whole life that the ideas in this book are dedicated.

As such, they are ideas firmly in contradiction to those which appear to be based on an analogy between nervous systems and computers on the one hand, between children and laboratory rats on the other. We want to make this very clear at the beginning. Sometimes, when we get to talking about the prepared environment or the ways in which children use learning materials, you may think we've gotten lost in the fascinating world of gadgets. We haven't. In the foreground are the marvelous children, each working in his own way to find out who he is in the world; and it is how these unique human beings make use of the equipment that tells us whether it's worthwhile or not.

Our second big reason for writing this book is that we know many people who at one time or another have wanted to start schools. It's not surprising: as parents we're concerned about the education of our children, and we'd like them to have the best. Philosophically committed to public education, ready to vote higher salaries for teachers and funds to improve buildings, we may yet have found the public schools overcrowded and underequipped, slow to change with a changing society, apparently unable to cope with the particular and individual needs of our own children. So the history of the Early Learning Center may be instructive.

There are other reasons for the book. I'd like to start people thinking about what's happening to preschool education. I'd like them to consider the differences between a school where children teach themselves and each other and a school where a dedicated teacher is seizing every opportunity to teach, teach, teach — making a lesson out of each moment's activity, attaching a learned concept to even a slight change in the weather. I'd like them to think about order: where it comes from, who makes it and how, what it means in a child's life; and then to compare a school where learning is the creation of order to one where order is imposed by a teacher, or — less usual in public schools, but all too common in those privately run — to a school where it has been decided that real learning can happen only amid a kind of hectic, often aggressive, always noisy confusion. I hope people will think about how children as well as adults become bored, and what the sources of boredom are, and how boredom relates to real freedom and to freedom's empty imitation, laissez-faire.

A more pressing reason: I'm worried — no, frightened — by the commercial prepackaging of preschools. Several large corporations, no one of which has had any previous connection with the education of young children, are reported to be going into the education business. You buy a franchise — a protected territory, a quickie training session for your staff, a day-by-day, minute-by-minute schedule, a layout for your school, and an assortment of materials clearly labeled for use with children of a specific age at a particular time in the schedule. This seems to me criminal. If a prepackaged cake mix doesn't rise, you can send the empty carton back to the manufacturer with a good chance of getting your money back, and no damage done. But educators are not talking about the damage a franchise holder might do to real children by following a prepackaged preschool program designed to meet the theorized average needs of some nonexistent Dick and Jane.

No — a good school happens when there is a personal interaction between deeply caring teachers and the very special, very individual children with whom they are working. A good school is unpredictable: it is created day by day in that interaction. It changes constantly; it is an environment responsive to the resources both teachers and children contribute to it. Far from a ready-made program for packaged people, it is a place where separate persons, children and adults, learn from and with each other as they use and build and remake that environment.

Because each school is different — and because good schools are continuously created from the interaction among teachers and children and environment, and are thus never the same from week to week or year to year — whatever we say in this book about the Early Learning Center can't serve as a blueprint for people who want to start schools of their own. But think for a moment about the difference between a blueprint and a conceptual model. We would like to suggest to you not only ideas about education but ideas about starting a school, and for that the history of the Early Learning Center may indeed serve as a model.

I began with my own needs. I wanted a good school for my own two boys. I asked myself whether my needs were unique, and found they weren't — other people in the community felt similar needs. So I set about meeting those needs: first, by getting training I lacked, then by finding a schoolroom and buying equipment. Then I put an ad in the local newspaper.

As easy as that . . . and as hard as that. You can do it, too — if you need to do it and, more importantly, if your need coincides with a lack in the community. You can start a good school if you begin with — and continue to evolve, unafraid to develop and change — a consistent philosophy of education: what you believe learning is, how it happens, what its place in the world is and must be. You can start a good school if you can and will express your philosophy in every detail of your school — in actions and objects, procedures, attitudes, your moment-to-moment behavior with children and teachers. You can do it if you're willing to devote a major part of your daily life to the job and to your continuing education for the job.

New schools — started by people like you and me — are appearing all over the country. Some of them are models of the best in education. A number of them have been accepted by state departments of education as just that: examples in action of new and better ways of educating children, to be visited and studied by teachers and school administrators. But other new schools struggle against a variety of problems. One school director finds it hard to get the right kind of equipment. Another discovers that what had seemed generous space is crowded when furniture, children, and teachers move in. One school is a constant battleground of ideologies. Many schools face perennial deficits. A few encounter legal trouble for failing to meet arbitrary state or municipal standards.

Every year a few new schools close, after a few months, a year, sometimes a number of years of operation. In some cases the closings are appropriate — the need a school was opened to meet is no longer pressing, or the school failed to provide good education for the children who attended it. But too often schools close which ought not to — and many have problems they ought not to have. One purpose of this book is to help keep those schools alive by suggesting ways in which they might be more effective.

We hope that what we have to say is of value. We hope it can help people who work in or are starting schools to conceptualize how children learn and what a good learning environment is. We hope it can help teachers help children.

Now a few words about the book itself. It is the product of a lot of note taking over the seven years of the school's history, attempts to put down on paper the purposes and procedures of the school. Much of it comes from the studying and thinking I did when I went back to college. It began to emerge in my mind as a book a couple of years ago because people kept telling me I should write one. A year ago I went through the drawer full of typed pages and put together a rough manuscript.

Interesting and important materials, said the editors of Little, Brown and Company, but not a book. Could I find someone to help me make a book out of it? I mentioned the problem to Will Hamlin, dean of the Adult Degree Program at Goddard College, through which I was just completing my B.A. To my surprise and delight he said he'd like to have a try at it himself. The outcome is this collaboration.

We've tried to make the school and its ideas come alive for you by writing about them in terms of specific children. They're real children, who attend the school now or who attended it in the past. Because we care about them, we've changed their names and some other identifying characteristics to save them and their parents embarrassment. We've concentrated on a few children because we think their life at the school reveals much that goes on there; but every now and then we'll mention a child you've not met before. Children are blessedly unique: a few of them may suggest the character of the school, but only all of them could tell the whole story.

We could list enormous numbers of persons to whom we are indebted, beginning with the children, who are very precious friends. We would add parents — persons who first entrusted their children to the Montessori School of Stamford, who lived with the school as it evolved into the Early Learning Center, who sold the ideas behind the school to their friends. We would add to the list those people who have been able to be generous with funds: they have helped us keep tuition fees low enough to make the school available to children from a wide economic spectrum.

We must also be eternally grateful to the Educational Facilities Laboratory, funded by the Ford Foundation, for helping us design the school and make a film about the building, and for providing funds for distributing the film to educational television stations all over the country.

But now let us come to dedications.

First, the children you'll meet in the book.

Second, Egon Ali-Oglu, architect and educator, designer of the school building, sharpener of our thinking, shaper of the school in more than its physical form.

Third, two very important people. My mother, Margaret Ferguson, and Will Hamlin's mother, Hilda Hamlin, don't know each other. They're a generation apart, from different backgrounds. But they are much alike in one way: out of their deep commitments to good education in the fullest sense of the word — growth towards ever more informed, concerned, active membership in human culture — they have fostered in each of us a fundamental concern for how children learn, what it is to teach, and how schools can be places for creative living. They deserve far more honor than this brief mention can give them; but then, neither of them lacks in the honor and love of her children and grandchildren and her many, many good and great friends.

Last (and first and always), my sons and Will's son: for each of us our most essential teachers about what children are, and how inseparable a part of living and growing is the business of learning.

Ralph Woodward was our editor at Little, Brown, cheering us on and suffering our (and his) delays. A number of people read some or all of the manuscript and made helpful comments, particularly Alice Blachly and Corinne Mattuck, of the Goddard College staff, and the Early Learning Center teachers.

TO START A SCHOOL

One

Morning

I get up early on school mornings. In the winter it's still dark here in Connecticut, but I want to be at the school at least an hour before the children arrive, at nine. It's chilly as I walk the country path between my old house, at one corner of our four acres of New England farmland, and the beautiful school building, which hugs the ground in an adjacent corner. I like the school at this time of morning, dark gray against lighter gray. As I come closer, its many floor-to-ceiling windows seem darker still. Then I see through them the windows at the other side of the large room which is the school.

This is my time for bridge building, as I've come to call it. The bridges are between one school day and the next — between what happened yesterday and what may happen today. Derek, for instance, two and a half, spilled the cutout letters on the floor just before clean-up time yesterday, and didn't know how to put them back. I wonder about this kind of apparently random play: is he on the verge of doing something with the letters, or were they just another kind of block to build with? Or was it simply random activity, the result of tiredness and boredom? I decide to make a point of the letters today with him: to sit with him for a while and ask him if he'd like to make some words with me.

I'm shivering a little with the morning cold as I unlock the school door. I hate locking it: I'd like the school to be a place always open, part of the community, to be used as individuals and groups need to use it. But that's not practical in a New England city in the 1970s. For perhaps the twentieth time I wonder what education could do to make a world where locks were never necessary.

It's quiet inside. I talked a lot about sound conditioning with Egon, our architect, when we were planning this lovely, remarkably inexpensive building. I don't know just how he did it. I do know that a group of children can be doing something noisy in one part of this big T-shaped room and hardly be heard in another part of it. Yet it's not like being in one of those deadly television or radio studios where every sound is absorbed and you feel as if something terrible had happened inside your head. The Early Learning Center is by contrast a very alive place — alive but quiet.

It's very quiet but full of life at seven forty-five, this winter morning. The life is in the learning materials. They speak quietly of concepts and skills and processes from their established places on the low shelves — wide boards on cement blocks. What each says is emphasized by the space around it — its psychic space as I think of it, identifying it as something separate and special. Some pieces of equipment ask for more of this space than others, so some shelves have only three or four items, separated by a foot or more of bare shelf. Some pieces, on the other hand, proclaim themselves more stridently, and six or seven of them occupy a shelf together. Most of the materials are on the shelves where they belong. We have clean-up time at the end of the day. The children are very good about it, so much of the straightening and arranging I do is unnecessary — except that it reacquaints me with objects and their uses, pieces of equipment and their relation to these children this day. But sometimes we ask a child to leave out materials he's been working with if he's in the middle of something we think he may want to continue.

So it was yesterday with Adam and the Montessori red rods (square sticks varying in size from ten centimeters — almost four inches — to a full meter — nearly forty inches — and painted a dark, Victorian red). He'd built a maze, a kind of square spiral or Greek key, and he was tiptoeing through it, trying not to touch the sides. Now I see the maze, a little awry, dark red against the gray rug. I straighten its sides and think about Adam. He's a black child, three years old, from an impoverished background — one of our scholarship children. When he first came to the school he was somewhat at a loss, perhaps stunned by the freedom, the busy children working at tasks they'd chosen for themselves, the teachers who watched or sat on the floor with one or several children, talking, helping, moving on to others. I saw Adam watching all of this, not knowing quite what to make of it, I suppose. One day a couple of weeks ago he had seemed entranced by three children who were working with the red rods. I suggested that he could use them too. He said nothing and did nothing just then, but an hour later he was busy with them, and now they're very much his thing.

The maze he's built is quite precise in its engineering — at

5

each right angle he's reduced the length of the side by ten centimeters, making a path about eight inches wide. I wonder if he visualized it that way and then went about creating in tangible form the image in his mind, or if it just happened as he started with the meter rod and then used the others in order of descending size, as they're put away in their tray. I must watch him today, perhaps show him some of the other materials which have to do with relative size.

I move on into the art corner, straightening the shelves with the logical and mathematical materials on them as I pass. Looking at the clean table, I'm reminded that five-year-old Janie was using the paints yesterday. Of course she cleaned up beautifully, exercising the same care with which she introduces herself to visitors: "My name is Jane Peterson Wilder." The white enamel dishes in which we mix colors seem to have been polished. The brushes are laid out in a precise row, and there isn't a scrap of paper around. (Did she throw her paintings away or take them home? Bruce, the high-school boy who helps us keep the building in order, has emptied all the wastebaskets, so I can't check. Next time she paints, I must watch.) Janie has been one of our problems. The bridge we have to help her build isn't from one day to the next so much as it is from her intelligence — manifest in everything she does — to freedom from the rigid perfectionism she's developed. For she is the prized and expected-to-be-perfect-in-everything daughter of parents for whom order, precision, cleanliness, and neatness are household gods.

Our problem is with them, the parents, as much as it is with Janie, of course. Fortunately, they are enthusiastic — if sometimes critical — supporters of the school. Less fortunately, they seem to understand little of its aims and methods. The main thing that pleases them is that Janie will enter first grade in the public school next year well ahead of first-grade level in reading and arithmetic.

A month ago I'd noticed her using the Montessori color

tablets, those beautiful two-by-three-inch wooden rectangles in subtle colors. There are eight hues, ranging from pale to intense, of each of six colors; the task is to shuffle them, then sort them by families, then grade them by intensity — for instance, from a misty early-spring-leaves green to a warm and strong apple green. Like many of the Montessori materials, they can be used in other ways, too — you can match intensity against intensity across the six colors or (if a Simon-pure Montessorian isn't watching) make colored designs or use them as thin, colored building blocks by setting them on their wooden edges.

Janie used them exactly as my Montessori training prescribed that they should be used. (Again and again she has determined what various materials are "supposed" to be used for, so that she can do what she then believes is the right thing.) She'd shuffled, matched, and graded the tablets over and over again, perfectly each time, without a glimmer of pleasure or satisfaction. After some weeks of watching this, I asked her if she'd ever used the paints.

"Yes."

I remembered — it had been at least a year ago.

"We still have them. They're over there if you'd like to use them."

"I don't mind."

That irritating New England answer. Does it mean yes or no?

"You could make colors like the tablets on paper, and cut them out and take them home."

"All right."

My error. I was suggesting one rigidity as a substitute for another. She did exactly what I'd suggested. She carefully mixed colors from the big jars of bright tempera, washing the brushes to keep the colors from getting muddy, amazingly enough keeping her hands clean. And made one set of color gradations after another. Was she dissatisfied with each set so that she had to make another, in the effort to create something quite perfect? Or was this just another exercise in precision, to be repeated for its own precise sake? I wondered again whether she took one or all of them home, or carefully folded them in half, tore them into quarters, and deposited them in the art corner wastebasket.

At least she'd used the paints. Maybe today she'll do something else with them. With any pleasure? Can we get through to her that learning is an exciting thing, full of the joy of discovery, deeply satisfying? Can we help her discover that order is something you create for yourself because it makes sense out of things, not something you copy apathetically or struggle compulsively to hold on to? Time's running short. Unless she's very lucky, the first grade she'll enter next fall will reinforce her perfectionism rather than modify it.   .

I find her problem a disturbing and typical one. Disturbing, because learning happens in both work and play — in both careful, precise effort and spontaneous gaiety — and so often educated families seem to stress one side or the other, rather than that wholeness in which both occur easily and appropriately. Typical? Of this part of New England, anyway, where the educated middle class is made up of engineers, architects, editors, commuters to Wall Street — persons who have chosen or have been chosen by occupations where a kind of rigid perfectionism is an important asset. A child like Janie is the innocent, disturbing, typical victim of this subculture. I make a mental note to talk to her parents again.

The time passes as I move about the quiet room, dusting a little, perhaps just as an excuse to touch various learning materials, moving some of them, straightening others. A set of jigsaw puzzle maps wasn't put away yesterday; I assemble the maps and put them on the shelf they've lived on for so long. (Some materials come and go as the children need them or lose interest in them, but the formboard maps seem always to be of interest.) The smallest square is missing from a set of bright plastic squares with raised edges designed to teach a child that smaller can always go within larger but larger can never go within smaller. Perhaps it does teach this concept; at any rate, the children enjoy taking the squares out and putting them back, and the colors are pretty. Another mental note: find the missing yellow square, or buy or make another one.

Many of the things I touch are the old familiar Montessori materials I learned about in my training and spent so much of my small capital on when I started the school. By and large they're wonderfully thought-out pieces of equipment — well made, a little old-fashioned in their polished-wood-and-brass-knob appearance. I love them, and the children learn from and with them. (I can't in good conscience, though, insist that they be used with the almost ritualistic exactness of detail demanded by the solemn disciples of the disciples of that great, inventive, concerned, enormously generous woman.)

Other materials are more recent discoveries — learning aids developed for the Leicestershire schools in England, which I brought back from my visit to Leicestershire a couple of years ago. They're handsome, brightly colored, lighter in look and feel than the Montessori materials. I find them most effective in helping children learn arithmetical logic. Many of the books come from England, too: small, inexpensive volumes, pleasantly illustrated, written in language which respects a beginning reader's intelligence and avoids the studied cuteness and overwhelming dullness of so many American books for children.

Then there are the school's own discoveries. Several times a year I visit the plastics and electronics surplus stores on Canal Street in Manhattan. The sign maker's alphabet case I found there — a plastic tray with inch-and-a-half-deep indentations in the shapes of the letters — we use to store the cutout cardboard letters. Alan, wanting to spell his own name, has only to look for a pocket shaped like an L for the second letter. He finds it in relation to the alphabetical sequence; when he's finished he will put it back, by again discovering a pocket shaped like an L, again in the order of the alphabet. Using the case, many children learn the alphabet without knowing they've learned it, particularly if another child helps with such cues as "it comes after the K." (Who ever defined one child helping another as cheating? It's one of the most effective kinds of teaching that can happen in a school.)

I bring back other things from Canal Street that I think may be useful: inch-high letters sandblasted on to uniform rectangles of thick, clear, Plexiglass; five pounds of inch-to-an-edge clear plastic cubes; wastebasket-size smoky plastic tubs to use for storing the Leicestershire Unifix cubes (hollow plastic, about an inch to an edge, interlocking). Good learning materials are everywhere, if you have the imagination to see them — or, perhaps, if you can break out of that conceptual cork-lined room in which only the curriculum experts attached to a university department of education can say what is good learning material and what is not.

While I've been putting things in their places, dusting, musing about the children and the materials, other members of the staff have been arriving. Shirley is a school parent, a member of our teachers' workshop last summer, especially interested in the arts and in movement. Carrie is the wife of one of our trustees, a warm and accepting woman, much concerned about the children's feelings. This year she is serving as an intern teacher. Isobel is our aide; in a few minutes she'll be busy with coats and overshoes as the children arrive. Barbara is an apprentice teacher from a nearby college. And Carol is the school secretary.

Peter, who teaches the new, small six-to-nine-year-old group, comes in to search through the supply shelves for wire and wood, then leaves for my house, where he's meeting these older children. One day soon, when we can find the money, the school will have a second-story addition for this group; meanwhile, we make out in temporary quarters. I remember that Peter and I have a conference with Egon, our architect, this afternoon, to talk about the addition. Egon, I predict, will stay on long into the evening, talking about education and the shapes that help it happen — it's a real passion with him, as this lovely building testifies.

Just before nine, the children begin to arrive. We greet each one by name and try to do a little more than that — a look in the eye, a word or two about something the child's interested in: an expression of our real pleasure that this particular child is with us this morning. Alice goes directly to the reading corner, after she and Isobel have dealt with her multizippered snowsuit. She's just four. She loves books and spends a lot of time with them, and I think she's on the verge of reading. Irene and Melissa stand in the middle of the room talking about the puppies each of them got for Christmas; then, almost without looking, Irene reaches down — still talking — to take out the blue plastic molded alphabet case with the cardboard letters. Adam goes over and stares at his red maze, walks through it twice, then thoughtfully kicks it apart and squats down to make a new one. Janie hasn't come yet, and I wonder for a moment if something's wrong; but just then she arrives, a little breathless, says a polite "Hello, Mrs. Skutch, I'm sorry I'm late" (by all of three minutes!) and walks-not-runs to the cloakroom. One absentee — Shirley's daughter, who has a bad cold. That makes fifty-three children from two years to almost six in this one room. I'm amazed all over again at how uncrowded it is, how quiet it is.

The children are busy. So are we. The day's begun.

Two

What It's All About

When visitors come to the school, they often begin the morning behind the one-way vision screen. From the middle of the school, it looks like a large mirror at one end of the room. Through the screen a visitor can see everything that's going on in the big schoolroom, without, he feels, disturbing the children. The children all know the secret of the mirror — each of them has at one time or another peered through it at the dimmed and objectified image of the familiar room. They're used to visitors, too. So the screen is mainly for the visitor's comfort.

Such observation usually doesn't last very long. The Early Learning Center is a friendly, active, busy school. The atmosphere is seductive, and soon a visitor may come from behind the mirror to sit on the gray carpet with one or several children, watching or helping. The children welcome men visitors particularly — they may see little of their commuting fathers except on weekends, and their teachers are mainly women. A man who sits down with a group of youngsters soon has Duggie climbing on his back, Irene nestling beside him, Alice running up to ask him to read a story with her.

I used to worry about these visitors. I tried to keep them behind the screen, with comfortable chairs and a tape-recorded commentary about the school piped into earphones. Unconsciously I regarded the school as my private preserve. But keeping visitors away from the children contradicted my commitment to freedom, and I knew that by working with the children these interested people could learn a lot more about the school than they could from my taped comments.

So many of my visitors end up as temporary teachers. I've learned a lot from them. Sometimes, I'll admit, the learning is negative — things I'll try very hard to avoid doing, like pouncing on a child who's happily building a house of blocks to shove at him the fact, long ago obvious to him, that two four-inch blocks are the same length as one eight-inch block. Most of what I've learned is positive, however: in particular, a kind of "listening with the third ear" to what children are saying behind or beyond the spoken words, a characteristic of master teachers from whatever philosophical persuasion or kind of school, it seems to me.

Every now and then a visitor makes us think about things we need to think about. A journalist came to the school one day, watched for a while, came out from behind the observation screen to sit by a teacher working with a group of children who were making words with the cutout cardboard letters, and

— to his surprise — found himself alone with the children. That was the beginning of a busy morning, as he moved from group to group, sometimes with a child riding on his back, taking part in the full life of the school. At noon, he helped a little girl put on her raincoat, found a sweater which may or may not have belonged to the boy who vaguely claimed it, and then came to sit with the teachers at their lunch-and-work table, a flush door set on two great chimney tiles.

"What's it all in favor of?" he asked. "Is it just that you want to turn out four-year-olds who can read and five-year-olds who know the squares and cubes of all the numbers from one to ten?"

I had to think for a while. I'm used to talking with visiting educators, with the parents of children who are, or may be, in the school, or with people who might give us financial help. Usually we talk about freedom to learn and how children teach themselves and each other when they have freedom, and I show them some of the learning materials. Big, bold, brash questions don't come up.

But I think I know pretty well what the Early Learning Center is in favor of.

"We want children to be strong selves," I said. "That means having confidence in themselves. Using their natural curiosity. Going at things, even when they're very little, like researchers — how does something work, why is it here, what can I find out about it, what can I do with it. It means not giving up easily. Working hard because you want to. Being inquisitive. That sort of thing."

Carrie, the intern teacher, said, "Something more, too, I think. I want them to trust their own judgments and their own feelings. That's a big reason to keep us from making praise-blame statements. But I think we do need to let them know we care. Sometimes a child seems worried or sad or pulling back into himself. I don't want to pry about this, and trying to cheer him up isn't going to do any good. What makes sense for me is to show him I know about his feelings and accept them. And if he wants to talk, I'll listen."

Shirley thinks about children like the artist she is. "I hope we can help the children see the world with new eyes. Then they'll be ready to share their seeing with others and find out how it fits with the seeing of others. I guess I'd call that helping a child cultivate his imagination. More than that, use his imagination."

Peter came in during the conversation and we put the question to him. He thought for a few minutes. Then, "I think we're in favor of all the homely American virtues — cooperation, competence, responsibility, courage, conscience, freedom, etcetera. Things that get talked about a lot. But most schools, you know, can't go much beyond the talking — too much competition, too many tests, all of that kind of pressure John Holt talks about that makes children so anxious. Here we can do it, I think, just because those are pretty natural things — doing something as well as you can, for instance, or helping someone else learn something you already know. Kids want to do the best — everyone does, really; it's just a matter of helping."

I learn from my staff — so much, so often. Carrie's concern, Shirley's vision, Peter's faith. The school is to a very great degree those qualities in action.

The visitor was thinking about these things as we all were, and taking notes. Then he asked me if I could sum it up in a phrase, a couple of words, something you could put in a caption or a headline.

No. But nearly, perhaps.

" 'Quiet confidence' says a lot of it," I told him.

Later I thought more about it. *Quiet confidence.* I wondered if the visiting journalist had noticed Jan trying to spell out his father's name with those cardboard letters the children love so much. He was very intent, quite sure he could do it, but unable to find the first letter. Without any anxiety he asked me for help. I got the eight-inch-high acrylic plaque on which is glued the sandpaper letter **P** and sounded it for him and asked him to sound it — *puh, puh* — and trace the shape of the letter with his finger, feeling the rough texture of the sandpaper surrounded by the smooth acrylic background. Then he turned to the blue compartmented letter case, found the compartment shaped like a **P**, and went ahead, sometimes saying the sounds softly to himself, to lay out **E, T, E, R**. He looked at **PETER** for a moment, went quietly across the room to get a cracker from the supply that's always there, and ate it thoughtfully as he walked back to sit and look again at his father's first name. Then he got up and ran off to another part of the room. Later, another child carefully put the letters back into their shaped compartments.

I knew the journalist had noticed Michael working with the little plastic Unifix cubes. Michael had made a solid square. "How many do you have there?" the journalist asked. "Sixteen," said Michael, "four to a side." He wasn't boasting and he wasn't guessing, just making a statement of fact, quietly confident. Michael is barely five.

Another vignette: Marcia going to one of the four doors that lead out into our piece of countryside, peering at the autumn stubble and falling leaves, seeming to sniff the air. Happy at what she saw of her world, she turned away, took a book from one of the racks where they're displayed, and sat down to read to herself. The outdoors is important to her, and she often goes out to explore parts of it by herself. Today, just knowing that it was there and that she could go into it if she wanted to was enough.

And then Mark, sitting by himself at a table in the household corner, peeling potatoes, four of them, one after another, and carefully putting the peelings in the garbage can before wiping off the table. The peeled potatoes stood in a bowl the rest of the morning. I took them home to cook for dinner. The next morning I thanked him. He seemed a little surprised — potato peeling was for him an end in itself.

Quiet confidence. You learn what you live, said William Heard Kilpatrick. I see these children living in these quietly confident ways at the school, and I'm quietly confident that they're learning something that's of enormous importance.

A few weeks after the journalist's visit to the Early Learning Center, I was talking about it to a magazine editor and his wife (part of my never-ending campaign to let people know what we're up to at ELC). The wife asked — with some malice, I fear, for she'd spent the evening defending systematic drill and subject matter–centered schooling — "What's the curriculum for quiet confidence?"

That one I can answer easily. The answer is in three parts. First is freedom, freedom to learn. Children are inquisitive, fascinated with the world, eager to try things out, in need of making sense out of their experiences. Given freedom, they learn a great deal for and by themselves and with each other's help. This isn't to say they don't often need the help of teachers. They certainly do. But we have to be careful to give it in a way which doesn't abrogate their freedom. I hope I was helping Janie towards more freedom by suggesting to her that she might want to use the paints; I certainly would not have been doing so if I'd insisted, or even urged, that she act on my suggestion. Jan asked me to help him find the first letter of his father's name as a free act. This kind of thing goes on all the time — it's what keeps us busy each schoolday morning. But much of the time the children ask for no help and none is thrust upon them. They learn in freedom. One of the major things they learn is what it means to be free.

There is a corollary to this. The more adults stand over children, directing them, quizzing them, judging them, or chastising them, the less are the children likely to learn through their own curiosity and need. What they learn — and this is much, I'm afraid, of the learning that goes on in the kinds of schools the editor's wife was talking about — is how to deal with demanding and punitive adults.

The second part of the curriculum for quiet confidence is the prepared environment. We give a child freedom to learn. We also want to give him as rich, interesting, full, and challenging an environment to learn in as we can prepare for him. What I've called building bridges is part of preparing the environment — arranging the school each morning so that it provides some dynamic continuity with what was going on yesterday. So are my periodic visits to the junk shops of Canal Street in New York City, with their bins of obsolete computer parts, lenses, plastic and metal castings, colored wires, bright brass gears. When I'm in Cambridge I go to Design Research for a yard or two of a new Marimekko print to hang on the wall, another way of preparing the environment. (I used to think the children didn't notice these things; the prints and pictures and hanging mobiles were for my own aesthetic satisfaction. But one day a little boy looked up at me from the stepped blocks he was working with and said, "I think this is the most beautiful place in the world!" And I decided the high cost of Marimekko fabrics is no extravagance.)

The learning materials are the most important part of the prepared environment. I've mentioned them before, and they'll keep coming up. A lot of our after-school work is concerned with them. One Friday we'll decide to repaint the Bonnie Prudden large-muscle gym equipment in bright primary colors, giving the enamel a couple of days to dry hard. Another day we'll go over the number-concept materials piece by piece, noting that one of a set of concentric rings is missing and must be found or replaced; sorting out that cube that was missing from the set of graduated square steps from the Unifix cubes, with which it's likely to get confused; deciding that perhaps it's time to bring out the Montessori gold beads again — strung on wire in lengths from one to ten beads, assembled into mats of one hundred and pleasantly hefty cubes of one thousand — and perhaps putting away the Montessori brown stairs, which no one seems to have used for a couple of weeks.

The third part of the curriculum for quiet confidence is the staff. Maria Montessori described teachers as observers first and foremost, and I know how important it is for me to be observing what's going on in every part of the school — one reason for our open floor plan, with work areas denoted by the way the shelves are placed rather than by walls. Second, she said good teachers were servants to their pupils. The metaphor is a little obsolete today, and I prefer to think of a teacher as a gracious hostess who offers but does not urge, who creates, as undemonstratively as possible, a pleasant atmosphere and helps each guest to enjoy it. The hostess who observes, carefully and caringly — how very different a picture of a teacher that is, from the one conjured up by the editor's wife as she discussed discipline and direction, instruction and drill and examination.

The members of the staff are part of the curriculum because they help children make use of the prepared environment in ways which honor and enhance their freedom to learn. We do this with some success at the Early Learning Center, I think. We are very different persons, but we have some characteristics in common, and it is on these that our success depends.

First, we have a strong commitment to the freedom of the children. Second, we have a real liking and respect for children; we enjoy them and that makes it possible for them to enjoy us. Third, we have among us a lot of imagination and good sense, and we're all willing to work very hard to bring these things to bear on the school. Fourth, we've had a good deal of training in putting these qualities to profitable use in the school, we've had much general education of the kind that gives specific training a context of values and aims, and we have our day-to-day experience, continually examined and reconstructed at our lunchtime sessions and our Thursday afternoon staff meetings.

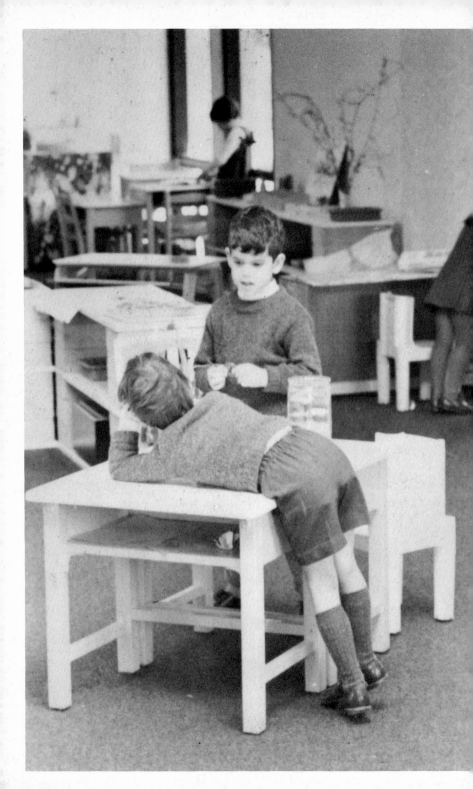

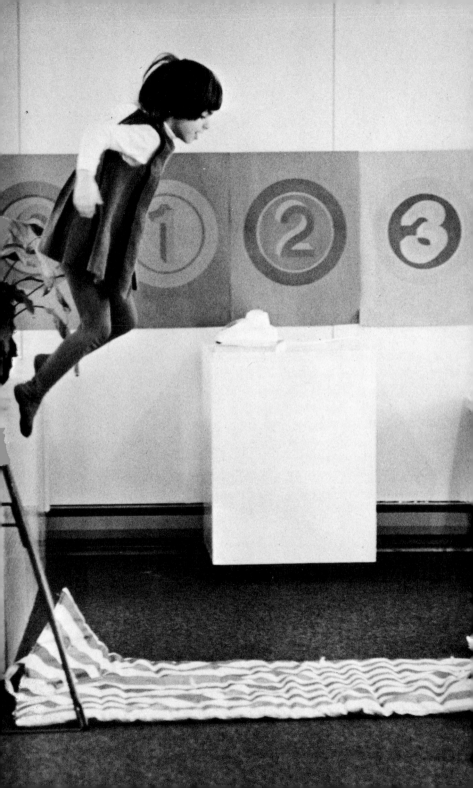

So that's the curriculum for quiet confidence: freedom so that a child can choose his own learning activities and build confidence by doing so; an environment prepared in such a way that there are a lot of things he can learn by exploring it on his own or with other children — quiet work because the environment doesn't generate competitiveness or frustration or boredom — and ourselves to help the children choose and use materials and activities.

I probably said it to the editor's wife far more briefly. I may have said it a little sharply, too. The kind of school she had been defending is totally alien to my ideas about what makes for good learning and thus for healthy, intelligent, contributing persons.

What I didn't say that night, because I thought Mrs. Editor wouldn't understand it, is that I think the heart of the curriculum is the learning materials themselves. They are the best self-instructional devices we can find. "Best" involves a number of criteria: they're effective ways of conveying various concepts; they do so in such a way that the concepts become part of the whole behavior of a child who uses the materials; they're of such a nature that it's clear what one can do with them and a minimum of introduction is needed; and they're intriguing, attractive, inherently interesting.

More than that, they're materials which lead to success. Most learning theorists are in agreement about one thing (however violently they disagree about other things!): you learn when you succeed at something. Failure, frustration, and anxiety, justified by some school people as realistic or necessary or inevitable, teach only the need for various neurotic escapes, and may even be physically damaging. (I'll never forget watching rats learn to avoid something painful, and shortly after, dying of stomach ulcers, and wondering about the psychosomatic diseases and how they might result from similar situations in human life.)

That learning materials should lead to success doesn't mean that they're toys or that they don't involve work. Making a slide with the Bonnie Prudden equipment involves a good deal of thinking about what boards and bars and standards to use, and a good deal of physical labor in putting them together. Often there's failure on the road to success — wrong thinking which has to be corrected, a heavy wooden bar put in the wrong notch in the metal standard early in the game, so that various parts have to be removed before the bar can be put in the right place.

When Jamie and Ann Louise work on this together, all of the complexities of shared labor come up — who's in charge (Ann Louise, without a doubt), who's more skillful at moving and positioning large and heavy materials (an even draw), who visualizes structures more clearly (Jamie by a long shot, something very hard for Ann Louise to admit). With these complexities playing their part, it's important that the shared work leads, after not too long a time, to a usable slide. It's important, too, that Jamie and Ann Louise have done it themselves.

It's because the materials aren't toys that I resist the verb "play" in talking about them. "Work" has a better sound to me. But work or play, it's the activity of learning. Each piece of equipment is designed around some particular way of dealing with the objects and processes that make up the experienced world. The red rods, for instance, are one of a number of learning materials concerned with quantity, proportion, and the relations of one quantity to another. The cylinders teach the way dimensions vary — how you can vary one dimension while holding others constant, or vary two dimensions at a time. Other materials teach such logical principles as congruence, similarity, the relation of container to thing contained, the nature of mathematical sets.

Another group of materials has to do with reading. Very basic are the Montessori sandpaper letters, which help a child get the shape of a letter by feeling it as well as seeing it, the cutout cardboard letters, and our big library of picture books, beginner's readers, and good children's stories. (A child who has taught himself to read moves very quickly from the primers to the stories, skipping many of the steps teachers of reading commonly lead their pupils through.) There are lots of other materials too: Lotto games; little books of pictures of objects all of which have names beginning with the same letter; the cards with which we play concentration (pairs of pictures, words, geometrical symbols, numbers, twenty or so different pairs to each set); and so on. Carrie works with the children in creating another kind of learning material, taking down stories from their dictation to read aloud to them and the other children.

Then there are the sensory materials designed to help children discriminate in various ways — the color tablets Janie was sorting and grading, for example. Shirley spends a lot of time working with the children on musical sounds and patterns, textures (metal, sand, play dough, spaghetti boiled to a wonderful stickiness), and taste and smell (elementary cooking and flavoring — Jell-O and junket and cookies with different spices and extracts in them).

The household corner has materials for domestic tasks — preparing simple foods, like Mark's potato peeling; lacing and tying shoes, with the help of one of the best-known Montessori aids, the front part of a high-laced shoe nailed to a board. There is a sink to wash dishes in, brooms and mops and sponges to clean with, and plastic aprons to tie oneself into.

Other related learning materials are simply part of the school itself: the low hooks in the coatroom, each marked with a child's name and some symbol he can associate it with; child-size toilets and child-height washbasins. The painting and clay tables in the art corner really need scrubbing at clean-up time. And the little ones really need the help of the bigger ones in getting in and out of snowsuits or raincoats, boots or rubbers. All of this is part of learning quiet confidence in oneself as part of the world.

Finally, there are the small-muscle and large-muscle activities and materials. Many of the logical and sensory materials need —

and help children develop — small-muscle coordination; some precision in placing blocks or using a brush becomes habitual. The basic material for large-muscle development is the Bonnie Prudden gym set I've spoken of several times: metal standards a yard high with a variety of boards, poles, bars, and rails which will fit into them to make balance rails, seesaws, bridges, slides, and so on.

But just as important is movement, of and by itself. The children run outdoors, follow each other single file along the stone fence, dig in the sandpile or the harder earth of the big field. Shirley or another of us or one of the children calls for follow-the-leader, and off we go — leaping, crawling, hopping, running, dancing around our four acres. And at the end of the day, indoors again, Shirley leads games in the Forum, a carpeted conversation pit backed by the big, mirrored one-way vision screen: Simon-says, the-bear-came-over-the-mountain, and other games which ask of the children all sorts of body responses.

There's the heart of the curriculum: a prepared environment and what children do with it. From it comes great confidence, quiet and not so quiet: the confidence to run and jump and dance; to build and paint; count, compute, figure things out; read letters and words and then books. From it comes solid learning, such that ELC children go into other schools well ahead of grade level in the basic skills.

It adds up, I think, to good living and good learning now, the best basis for good living and good learning later on.

Three

Children at Work

In the first two weeks of the school year, we bring new children into the Early Learning Center a few at a time for a short day's introduction. A number of children who have been at the school before are there to meet them and help them. I've visited all of the newcomers in their homes, some of them several times, and I greet each of them in the most welcoming way I know, talking to the boy or girl as an individual, not just one of many new faces.

I or one of the other teachers — and often an older child or two — take the new child on a tour of the building. We want him to know where the bathroom is (and that he's free to go there whenever he needs to, without asking — something particularly important for two-year-olds). We want him to see the practical-life corner, the paint and clay corner, the gym set (the older children and I have made something with it — a seesaw or a slide, perhaps), and the shelves with the learning materials ready on them.

I choose one or two things from the shelves to show a new child. Often it's the Montessori cylinder blocks, brick-shaped, foot-long pieces of polished hardwood, each drilled to hold several smooth wooden cylinders with handy knobs on top — cylinders which vary only in their diameter in one block, only in their length in another, and in both length and diameter in a third. Very young children like to take the cylinders out and put them back in: they fit closely enough to make a tiny sigh of escaping air as they settle into place. Or I show a child the Unifix cubes of brightly colored plastic, so made as to fit together in rows or platforms or structures. They make a nice snap when you push them together or pull them apart, and a fine "plop!" when you drop them into those smoky plastic bins from Canal Street where they're kept. I tell the children they can work with these materials or any others, and that we'll be glad to help.

Sooner or later, as the weeks go by, a situation is likely to arise in which I'll tell each new child my version of the traditional nursery-school rule: I can't let you hurt yourself, other children, the learning materials, or the school. But I don't make a routine of saying this the first day or announcing it as a general rule; outside the context of a real situation it would be threatening and meaningless. In a real situation — a child stepping on the plastic Unifix cubes, for instance — the rule makes demonstrable sense and is likely to be accepted and remembered.

The weeks do go by, faster than we realize until we stop and look back to those introductory days. As I write, we're ten weeks into the year. Thanksgiving has come and gone — without, I may say, a single cutout crayoned turkey being pasted to a window. (Nor will we have the Christmas trees and Santas, hatchets and hearts, chickens and bunnies and eggs kindergarten children all over the country seem fated to reproduce every year.)

I look back at my daily notes on the children to see what's happened, what's being learned, so I can tell you something about the Early Learning Center in action. Three of the children seem to represent much of what goes on here. I won't call them typical, because they're unique; but they will serve as illustrations.

Danny is one of the youngest children, now two and a half. He came to the school this September very bright and eager, and I enjoyed introducing him to a lot of materials and activities. He wanted to try everything. My notes show that he's tried a lot, perhaps everything he's ready for at this age.

One thing he did deserves special comment. Maria Montessori made much of practical-life activities, aware that young children — twos and threes in particular — have a great sense of order and cleanliness. A lot of the materials and activities she made use of in helping children turn this seemingly innate characteristic into a repertory of useful skills are obsolete today. Others have become encrusted with ritual. But a central truth remains: as many a patient and loving mother has discovered, a three-year-old really can help with the dishes or fold the towels for the linen closet, and learn something about the discipline of materials and his own control over them in the process.

It was scrubbing the tables that caught Danny's interest. (This is one of the Montessori activities that has become ritualized. The seventeen steps to proper table scrubbing taught to me during my Montessori training embarrass me now, and

I'm sure they would bore a child as active and inquisitive as Danny.) Since he seemed interested in the practical-life corner when I took him there on that first-day tour of the school, I simply moistened a cloth, rubbed it over the porcelain enamel top of the kitchen table there, and said, "One of the things you can do is help clean off the tables. You scrub them with a wet cloth, like this, and then dry them with a dry cloth, like this." A couple of weeks later I noticed him doing just that, so I showed him how to wash out the cloths and hang them up to dry when he was finished. Since then, scrubbing tables is something he's turned to regularly, at least once a week.

I hold no brief for table scrubbing for the sake of table scrubbing. You scrub a table when it needs to be scrubbed. But a two-year-old sees it differently. Just as Mark was peeling potatoes without any apparent concern for their future in my stewpot, so Danny likes to scrub tables whether they're crying out for it or not. He's learning by doing — not just how to scrub tables, an activity of no world-shaking importance, but how to do a job thoroughly, thoughtfully, well.

One more point about this somewhat pointless activity. I introduced Danny to table scrubbing at the same time that I was showing him a lot of other things: one of those big English picture puzzles made up of large parts with sensible outlines (a whole face is a single part, for instance); the Unifix cubes; the cylinder blocks. It was he, not I, who chose table scrubbing as one of his particular activities. The teacher as hostess: I offer various possibilities, but I don't urge, cajole, demand, or manipulate. The child makes the choices, and I respect his freedom to do so.

What Danny's spent most of his time with recently, though, is the tub of Unifix cubes. Like many good learning materials, they can be used in a variety of ways. Danny was beyond the stage of just emptying the tub out on the rug and then dropping the cubes back in one by one to hear that satisfying "plop!" He discovered how they connect together (perhaps another child showed him) and started making sticks of five, six, ten blocks. Then he got the idea of making trains — long lines of blocks connected together so that moving one of them moved them all. His trains grew from two feet to six; and finally one day, with mounting excitement, he built a train which reached all the way across the room, from the sunny reading bay on one side to the main entrance on the other. Great discovery, great triumph!

Two things about this triumphant discovery: First, it depended on there being enough Unifix cubes. Often children don't have enough materials — at home or at school — to do anything that isn't limited or constrained. If you're buying blocks for your child, buy a big set. If you're involved with a school, make sure you have enough of everything so that several children can work together without being cramped by a shortage of materials.

Second, it's important to realize what a two-year-old can learn by putting together enough Unifix cubes to reach from one side of the big schoolroom to the other. It means — as with scrubbing tables — he can do something big and succeed at it — that persistence pays off and patience is rewarding.

But more than this was going on. Using the cubes, Danny had come to a sense of pattern, sorting them by color and assembling them in groups of one or another color. His trains had red cars, blue cars, yellow and green and violet cars. Often he'd repeat a sequence: blue, red, yellow, blue, red, yellow. He was learning to turn the miscellaneous — a tub full of plastic cubes of assorted colors — into the orderly — a connected line of cubes of great length arranged by colors in patterns.

Danny is learning to count, too. Maria Montessori made a "spindle counting box" when, I suppose, Italian peasant women were still spinning wool by hand. We use ours for all sorts of objects (I change them frequently). The box has ten compartments, each marked with a large number. You put one spindle or button or bead or tile or whatever in the box marked 1, two in the box marked 2, and so on. Danny's used it for Unifix cubes. It's helped him become very sure of the lower numbers — he's got a real sense of fiveness by now. (I should add that he has apparently no sense of sixness yet. Children learn one through five from their own fingers; then they hit a plateau before going on to six through ten. There's far less of a plateau after ten.)

Danny's use of the spindle box illustrates how children learn many of the things in which they become competent. Leslie Hart calls the process random learning, not because there's no pattern to it but because the pattern is so individual and so dependent on circumstances. The spindle box was near the tub of cubes — not next to it but on a shelf nearby; it looked like something to put things in (like the empty honey pot Pooh gave Eeyore), and that's just what Danny did. He was ready for something more than just the nice hollow sound the cubes make — perhaps he had a notion that the various compartments and the symbols beside them meant something.

What happened? Another child may have happened by at the right moment and worked with him putting one cube in the 1 compartment, two in the 2 compartment, and so forth. Perhaps he'd just seen other children using the box with other objects. Maybe a teacher helped and forgot to record it. At any rate, it wasn't more than a few days after he took the box off the shelf that he was counting the right number of cubes into each compartment up to five.

John Holt has written about how this happens with older children: random play with a balance beam led, with no teacher help, to the discovery that one weight placed six inches from the fulcrum will balance two weights placed three inches from it on the other side, and so forth. He talks about how children worked with his electric typewriter, many wanting just to "make it go" but a few — those who were ready as a result of who knows what earlier experiences — using it to learn to write words and then read them back. Out of random activity come pattern and meaning. Any mother who can clearly remember her baby's first year knows this. Is it surprising that the way a child learns — so analogous in every way to growing — follows the same sequence?

Many of Holt's pupils weren't ready to carry the random exploration of the typewriter into the complex activity of reading. Similarly, not every two-and-a-half-year-old is as ready as Danny for making color patterns and counting. More girls than boys are ready for conceptual learning at two and a half, and the gap widens or is at least maintained for another dozen years or more.

That doesn't mean we keep most two-year-old boys out of the school; Jack is still pretty much of an infant, but I think he's absorbing a great deal just being here. One day, when our backs are turned, he'll start doing the kind of things Danny's been doing. We'll examine our notes to see whether there was any indication of a breakthrough in the making — and they will leave us still wondering: does the beginning of conceptual learning of the kind we're fostering in the school depend on a long and gradual preparation, or is it something that just happens as a child matures biologically and socially?

Alice is my second example of a child. She's in the middle of the two-to-five range, four and a bit. When she came to us at two and a bit, she was very much like Danny — into everything, wanting to learn everything. He's moved towards counting; she, on the other hand, moved early towards letters. I've spoken of her as an almost-reader. I mean by that that she still likes to be read to (so do most children and many adults) and isn't yet reading aloud to the younger children, as Ann Louise is, for instance. But she spells words easily with the cutout letters, and she loves to play word games.

Concentration is one of her favorite games. She's not alone in this; two or three or four children are playing it almost every day, often several groups in a day. I mentioned the materials earlier — pairs of cards with pictures, symbols, words, numbers on them, perhaps twenty pairs to a set. They're shuffled and then laid out facedown in some kind of pattern (a rectangle five cards by eight, for instance, if your set has twenty pairs). A child turns over one card, then another; should they by chance be a pair, he takes both of them; if they're not, he turns them back down and it's the next child's turn. As the game progresses, all of the cards get turned over, and a child with a good visual memory comes to know where many of them are. Alice turns one over — an ice-cream cone. She remembers the other ice-cream cone was in the bottom row, the third card from the left, turns it over, and takes the pair to put in front of her. It's a good game because you can move from pictures to abstract symbols to numbers or words without anyone minding: it's all the same process, seeing similarities and differences and remembering them. Alice came to like it best with words. There's no question that she sees the words as alike or different with great consistency, and that she remembers them enough to be able to locate the twin of BOY because Joey turned it up four turns earlier in his search for a mate to CAR. But she doesn't speak the words aloud, and I'm not a "And what word is that, dear?" teacher, so I can't say for certain how many of the words she's actually reading.

A game she loved last year but plays less often now is something we invented, the vowel game. We teach short vowel sounds — at, ebb, it, on, up — to begin with. For the game, I give each of five children one of the sandpaper-letter vowels. (The sandpaper letters are about four inches high, cemented onto eight-inch acrylic plaques; as a child traces a letter with his finger he gets kinesthetic information to reinforce his visual and aural learning.) Then I hold up pictures of objects with simple, one-vowel names.

A large cat.

"CAT — that's mine!" says Melita, who has the sandpaper A.

I hand her the picture.

A scatter rug, cut out of a Sears, Roebuck catalogue.

"RUG!" several of the children say. Alix, who is holding the sandpaper U, isn't sure about the short U sound, but when no one else claims it, she tries "Rug — ruh — ug," and she gets the picture.

We go through a number of letters. Alice has the I and gets "king," "hill," "lips," "fish." She says the lips are a smile, too, and that's also an I sound, which shows she's gone beyond the first vowel sounds.

Danny likes to sit in on this game though he's really not ready for it. Interestingly enough, the other children don't mind. When he misses the connection between the O he's holding and "pot" and "dog" and "log" and "mop," one of the others is likely to say, "That's Danny's." If they don't I do, sounding the word for him as I toss him the picture card — "puh-o-tuh," with the stress on the vowel.

I remember Alice's first use of the cutout letters. Random behavior again — she simply spilled them out on the floor and stirred them around, as if she didn't know what else to do with them. Sometimes she'd pick one up and bend it or twist it or tear it, and I'd have to say, "I'm sorry, I can't let you do that; the letters have to stay flat and in one piece."

This kind of thing happens regularly — the appropriate situation for the simple rules I mentioned earlier. But handling it isn't easy. I had to try to see that Alice didn't develop a negative feeling towards anything to do with letters — rather, that she understood that letters are good things, that using them is a good thing, but that there are some things one cannot do with them. In such a situation it has to be very clear that what's being talked about is the damaging of materials everybody uses, *not* naughtiness on the one hand or letters as forbidden objects on the other.

Out of which comes a general rule: talk to children about your own reactions to specific behaviors. I remember saying something like, "Danny, I like the way you've scrubbed that table — it's all clean for the next people who want to use it." I specifically did not say, "What a good boy you are to have scrubbed that table!" — which would have implied, among other things, what a bad boy you would have been if you hadn't, and taken the emphasis off the action to put it on goodness-badness. So, "I can't let you do that — the letters have to stay flat and all in one piece," or something of the sort, instead of, "Alice — stop that this instant! You know better than to bend the letters like that. Now leave them alone and go and play with something else." That kind of sharp statement, full of judgment and blame and anger, I hear all too often, not only in homes but on the part of harried schoolteachers.

Whether it was the way I handled it or just her own persistence, Alice went on with her random letter play without doing violence to the materials. Soon she was grouping together the letters that looked alike (inaccurately at first — the same confusions an apprentice printer suffers when he first faces a case of type and finds it hard to distinguish W from M, C from G, O from Q). She was also learning the letter shapes from the sandpaper letters. Often I carry a couple of them around with me as I move about the room. I'll sit down with a child who is between projects and ask him if he'd like to trace a letter. I try particularly to do this with children who are interested in letters, so Alice got a daily dose of it.

The sandpaper letters, the cutout letters, and the various word games all fed into each other for her. I invited her into groups where we were giving the right names to objects and pictures of objects. I showed her the little ring-bound books of pictures, all of which have names beginning with the same letter — the F book, the S book, the B book — and after going through one of them, we'd think of other words beginning with the same letter. After a while she began spelling out some of the words with the cutout letters. Then it was time to move to cards with somewhat more ambiguous pictures identified by full words printed out below them: a boy showing his bicycle to a girl and her dog (right out of Dick and Jane), identified by the word "bike," for instance.

This sounds like a sequential subject-matter curriculum, and indeed it is. But I have to point out two things. First, this was the Alice curriculum, not the Danny curriculum or the Melita curriculum — a sequence of activities unique to her experience in the school. Second, she chose this curriculum for herself from a lot of possible activities going on in the school. These were activities in which she found success and interest and pleasure (place those three words in whatever sequence you wish — they go together in learning). They were available in the school because we prepared the environment to make them available, in the belief that coming to terms with letters and words is something children want to do and need to do in this culture; but, like every child in the school, she had the freedom to make use of them or not. Freedom to learn involves freedom to choose from the very beginning.

Our role in her learning may clarify something of what teachers do in a school where a great deal of self-instruction is going on. During the two years that she was pursuing this very individual curriculum, she was also doing a great many other things; and much of the reading work I've described she did on her own. I was aware of it (one of the reasons I keep daily notes is to remind myself to observe all of the children each day) and I probably worked with her a few minutes almost every day. But mainly she was doing things by herself or with a group of other children, so my awareness was probably the most important aspect of my teaching. I open George Dennison's wonderful *The Lives of Children* quite at random and find him writing of how important it is to keep one's eyes on persons instead of losing oneself among issues. I think that's a key point in our teaching.

We are constantly aware, then, of a child working mainly on her own. Given the kind of freedom we work with at ELC, it's not surprising that Alice has complemented our awareness of her by being aware of us. She tells us firmly and clearly what she can do and what she can't. When she was matching pictures to written words she'd sometimes get into things that were too hard for her. She'd try for a while to work out a word with two vowels in it, one short and the other long, and then call out, to whichever of us was passing or nearby, "Hey, I can't do this, Mrs. De Clerque, I can't do this," and sometimes get quite agitated. Our usual answer to that was to steer her to simpler materials. (There's a box of pictures of things with short, easy, one-vowel names and a box with longer, more complicated words. Being the energetic child she is, always wanting to try something new, she was likely to pick the more advanced box). "There's another box here that might be more fun — let's try it. We can work with the other one tomorrow or the next day."

I could have used a lot of strategies with her to help her overcome the frustration of the difficult words, sitting with her while we worked on double consonants, assorted vowel sounds, the deviant spellings with little relation to phonetic sense that English is famous for. But I find I use these "teachery" methods less and less. With a rudimentary phonetic vocabulary, a child has enough of a beginning to learn the rest very much on his own, if he can be helped past the most frustrating roadblocks. After going back once or twice to the easier words, Alice began sounding out the difficult ones, and even words which the rules would suggest she ought not to know how to pronounce at all. Again and again children short-cut the rules when they're free to learn for themselves, at their own rate, in their own ways.

This year Alice is painting a lot. She's painted ever since she came to school, but it used to be an occasional activity; now it's more purposeful. I think her painting is getting more sophisticated, though I'd have trouble putting into words what I mean by that term. Technically, she certainly has more control over brush and colors: she can do in her paintings what she wants to do. She's also doing a lot of woodworking, which is brand-new for her. This may be because Jan is doing wood-working, and Jan and Alice have become a pair. Children often pair off at three or four or five; they become each other's teachers and protectors as well as companions.

I mustn't leave you with the notion that Alice is a little angel, about to fly away on wingèd words. There are times when she seems anything but endearing: the third time on a rainy morning (when the oppressive weather is getting to teachers and children alike) that she grabs my hand and says, "Will you read with me, Mrs. Skutch?" Or one of those moments when her frustration at not being able to do something beyond her ability comes out at full voice: "Mrs. Skutch, hey, Mrs. Skutch, I can't do this, I need help, please, Mrs. Skutch!" Or that day not so long ago when she and Jan decided to paint their own and each other's hands, faces, hair, and clothes — and before we knew it, a number of other children had decided it was a lovely idea.

(Shirley is a genius at turning things like that into something productive and wash-and-wearable, but she was away that day. I just had to wade in, shouting, "Hey — stop that. Stop it, I said!" None of the "I'm sorry, dear, I just can't let you do that," which I typically practice as well as preach.)

So consider Alice to be devil as well as angel, ordinary as well as extraordinary: in short, a whole person discovering and displaying her wholeness.

Ann Louise is my five-and-a-half-year-old among these living illustrations of the Early Learning Center at work. But first some comments on this older group.

They have a particular kind of problem. Growth is never even, of course, and there seem to be crisis points in the growth of children when the unevenness makes for real difficulty. Our almost-six children are impatient for activity of some important kind (what they will perceive as important). Careful learning is too slow now. Their ambitions race ahead of their abilities. I suspect they are able to conceptualize a great deal more than they can either say or do — as if conception was miles ahead of logic at this point. Out of frustration and irritation, or boredom, or some fear of attempting what they apprehend they will fail at — my guesses, but thoughtful ones — they may well regress into two-year-old activities, like block building or almost patternless play with Unifix cubes.

We need materials for them, suited to their developed skills but not asking of them a kind of thinking they can't yet do. Watching them deal with the Bonnie Prudden gym set, I've thought they might well build solid houses if they had life-size, lightweight Lincoln Logs. I think they're probably ready for simple printing, too, with big, easy-to-assemble type and a press which doesn't require fussy adjustment. I hope we can help in developing some of these materials over the next decade.

I hope we can also experiment with materials already developed but not yet in use with the young children. Videotape and audiotape are two such materials — ways an impatient child can get his message set down for himself and others without the painful labor of beginning writing. A little work has been done with typewriters; and that wonderful (and very costly) talking typewriter invented not too long ago — you will hear of its part in persuading me to start the school — has taught children to read and type at the same time. With or without typing, these children can certainly use that granddaddy of the duplicating machine, the tray of hardened gelatin called a hectograph.

It's often suggested that one way to help children deal with regressive behavior is to build something positive about it: the child who wants to go back to playing with blocks will help the younger children build, or be in charge of putting the blocks away where they belong; the child for whom water play is again important will be the school dishwasher or floor cleaner. And so on. I know this works when the child chooses it. But I'm chary of asking a child who is in a critical developmental stage to take responsibility for its own sake; it's probably one of the things he's most ambivalent about and thus one of the causes of the crisis. He must determine his role, not his teacher.

Ann Louise has been in this crisis stage. Last year she was very much involved in math, and doing very well at it. But this year she turned to block play, paint daubing — very aggressive, almost purposely ugly — and dressing up to be someone else who can make faces at her in the mirror. She still read and still did numbers, but the core of passionate interest that used to give energy to these activities seemed to have disappeared; they appeared to be escapes from boredom which shortly proved boring themselves. Her group play had always been very active; now what had been leadership turned into bossiness of a sometimes demanding, sometimes manipulating, kind.

In short, Ann Louise is a child you worry about: very bright, very adept, sharp, contradictory, and in some kind of turmoil which was making her difficult to have around. I write of her because she represented a problem, and you have to realize we have problems; and also because she's the prototype of the American middle-class child. This is to say, she's the victim of circumstances very common in this day and age, exaggerated for greater visibility by the exurbanite culture of this part of Connecticut.

My mother tells me that in her childhood, and even more so in her mother's childhood, middle-class children (and probably children from many backgrounds and social classes) had a strong sense of time and place — a continuity, a tradition. Out of this came some sense of secure identity, even in the face of such distressing social ills as war, depression, racism, and prudery. Today, for all but a few children that continuity and tradition are gone. Ann Louise's family, for instance, have lived in Stamford only the three years she's been in the school, and they talk now of moving to New Milford if they can get a decent price for their home. They live at the margin of their income — as destructive of tranquillity for a $30,000-a-year executive as it can be for a $6,000-a-year clerk.

Weekdays, Ann Louise knows her father only as a harried presence rushing through breakfast to catch a commuter train and an exhausted person arriving home desperate for a drink just as she's going to bed. Weekends he swims or plays golf or tennis, works his way through a briefcase full of stuff from the office, goes to a party or occasionally has one at his house, and naps a good deal. Her mother is both busy and bored, disconnected from the life her husband leads in New York, trying very hard to become involved in the life of the community. She has poked and prodded to find a place for herself — the March of Dimes, volunteer work at the hospital, a Great Books discussion group. The New England community soaks up her time and energy but remains impervious. Ann Louise bears the brunt of her mother's frustration.

To make matters worse, there are two sisters to compete for the attention of the parents, one of them just three, one a baby — family planning's response to the ubiquitous myth about the difficulties of only children, and, I suspect, the mother's attempt to find fulfillment in having babies. Ann Louise and Dulcy are in constant conflict over the crumbs of attention and caring their mother has left over from taking care of the baby. It's harder on Ann Louise than it is on Dulcy; Ann Louise had to watch Dulcy being babied and made much of two years ago, and now Dulcy vents on Ann Louise the jealousy awakened in her by the new baby's arrival.

So Ann Louise comes to school expensively dressed but needy at heart. I remember her blustering in one day, paying no attention to my greeting. She threw her pretty fur-trimmed coat on the floor, jumped on it, kicked it, then left it crumpled, and ran off to knock down a bridge Jeremy and Melita had built the day before with the gym set.

Carrie went over to her.

"Something's bothering you, Ann Louise."

No answer.

"Let's go pick up your coat, and then we can sit together."

A sound — part scream, part "Yah!"

"Come along, Ann Louise. We can walk outside for a while if you like." (Which, if it had worked, would have made a chance to start the day over again.) Carrie reached out her hand to Ann Louise, who was sitting on the floor, leaning against one of the gym-set standards, sucking her thumb. Ann Louise seemed not to have heard her.

Then Ann Louise got up, kicked the metal standard, and yelled, "Ooh — my foot hurts!" Carrie put a hand on her shoulder and they went over to the reading corner, where there's a big rocking chair. They sat together for perhaps a quarter of an hour, Carrie holding the little girl and stroking her hair, Ann Louise still sucking her thumb. Carrie spoke to her — probably something like "Are you ready to work now?" — and Ann Louise ran off to the Wendy House (playhouse), where, as far as I could see, she was being her usual bossy self, but perhaps a little more cooperative than she had been for some time.

I don't know whether Carrie did the right thing or not for Ann Louise. It's certainly a warm and human response to want to give affection to a child suffering from too little of it. Does it do more than ease the situation for the school — that is, does it really help Ann Louise cope with her existence and learn what she has to learn?

I can't say I had any greater success with Ann Louise than Carrie did. A child who throws temper tantrums brings out the worst in me. Let me tell you something *not* to do if you have a tantrum thrower in your schoolroom. I don't know what brought it on, but one day Ann Louise started screaming. Even in our sound-conditioned school, even in an open and free situation, screaming attracts attention. Children all over the room were looking on with some alarm. In a moment of silence

— perhaps Ann Louise was breathing — I said, "All right, let's have a screaming time — let's see if we can all scream as loud as Ann Louise!"

Some did, some didn't. I think a number of children were embarrassed. I think, too, that they knew Ann Louise was screaming about something real, and that it wasn't to be made fun of or turned into a game. Children take each other seriously and honestly. Instead of relieving the situation, I had increased the tension.

Two-year-old Marna came along one day and showed us what you can do with someone like Ann Louise. A tantrum was in progress — screaming, stamping, jumping up and down. Neither Carrie nor I saw anything we could do about it, and we were waiting for the storm to blow over. From some corner of the room came little Marna. She walked up to Ann Louise, took her by the hand and tugged at her. The screaming stopped in mid-shriek.

"Come on, Ann Louise," said Marna, "let's go get an apple."

Ann Louise looked at Marna. Then (seeming almost to shrug her shoulders) she went off with the two-year-old to look for one last windfall under the old tree by our south entrance. They found an apple, came in together, cut it up together, and ate it side by side.

Marna hadn't been a special friend of Ann Louise's, and it's not common in my experience that a two-year-old should move in so determined a way towards an almost-six. Something in Ann Louise must have reached out to Marna. Perhaps it was simply Ann Louise's competence. Perhaps it was her suffering. I doubt if even Marna knows.

The outcome? The tantrums stopped. One very busy day Carrie asked Ann Louise to help with the younger children: "You're the oldest one here and I need your help." Since then, Ann Louise has been reading to the little ones, helping them on with their overshoes and snowsuits, and enjoying it. She's still bossy at times, but in a way which seems to go well with her new role. I wait for the next tantrum, but it hasn't come yet. In a real situation, she has chosen the kind of responsibility I could not ask her to take just for its own sake.

Something else made a great difference in Ann Louise's life in the school. Late in the spring we built a special place in the north bay for the older children, to give them space where they could feel that growing up was worthwhile. Ann Louise came into her own as she explored this "inner space." We'll say more about the space when we describe the building, but here it's important to say that physical environment *does* make a difference, when it reflects the needs of children. Ann Louise is living proof of that.

I guess they're on their various ways to quiet confidence, these several children. Danny and Alice will probably run into difficulties at that critical age, but I don't think their problems will be as great as Ann Louise's; they won't, on the other hand, need as dramatic a resolution. As for Marna? She seems to be skipping happily along, like Dorothy on the road to Oz. Like Dorothy, she may pick up a stumbling wayfarer or two. I watch her with joy.

Four

Freedom to Be and Do

I have a fire burning in the fireplace tonight. The weather's trying to prove that though we're only an hour from New York, this is still New England — where March winds drive the snow, and spring never obeys the calendar. I grew up in Virginia where a snowfall was an extraordinary event. Winter was a short, brown time breaking a sequence of greens. The whiteness of New England winter, the gold and crimson fall, the waiting quality of early spring are still exciting to me.

It seems to me a good thing for children to grow up where there are marked seasons. Education involves change in a lot of ways. Among other things, education has to help children live in an environment which is changing constantly. The seasons are a good introduction.

Our school is purposely built with floor-to-ceiling windows and four doors to the outside to bring the outdoors into the life of the children. I'm shocked to see new school buildings going up in neighboring towns designed to do just the opposite — windowsills so high that a child sitting at his desk can see nothing but sky, shades and Venetian blinds so planned that even that sky may be excluded, entrance and egress formidable and guarded.

It's still summer when our school opens. There are flowers in the big meadow — asters and black-eyed susans, a few remaining daisies, lots of goldenrod, sunflowers, hollyhocks. The days are warm enough to run outside with a minimum of clothes. The hose is connected sometimes, when we can be on the lookout for too much mud.

Then we watch as the trees change, and the late berries come, and the birds begin turning in great flocks above our meadow. Shirley goes to Vermont for the weekend and comes back with a great armload of scarlet, crimson, gold — maple and sumac, oak and beech. Our own colors come later, more quietly, yellows and orange-browns, an overall feeling of gold. Marcia watches the birds swinging around the sky, begins to run in wide circles in the field, and then flops down, laughing, in a pile of leaves.

Then, quite suddenly, winter begins — mid-December usually, sometimes earlier. Snow becomes customary stuff. On blizzard days I look out the back door of this old house, built solidly so long ago against the exigencies of just such weather, and the school has vanished — nothing but swirling white.

Spring will come, I reassure myself, hearing the wind moan around the little porch at the back of the house. A Connecticut spring has a softness about it which the lush verdancy of Virginia hadn't prepared me for. Like many people, I have a religious feeling about the coming of new life. I take into myself the triumph of snowdrops and crocuses which seem to force open frozen ground, and tiny leaves feathering bare sticks seem truly miraculous, like Tannhäuser's staff coming into leaf.

Spring misleads me into verbiage. The children are wiser: when they shout their way happily down the greening meadow there are no words. Last spring I came on Duggie giggling a little as he squished his toes in the gooey bottom of a little pool left by a passing shower: it was a poem about spring, pared of its words.

In a sense the seasons are part of our prepared environment. When we were planning the building, Egon and I talked a lot about giving the children freedom to go in and out, about a heating system which wouldn't be upset by coming and going in all weather, about doors easy for children to open from either side but closing tightly against wind or snow or rain, about a rug which could take the dirt and wet of so much inning and outing. Thanks to this long-range preparation, the school environment is one in which children can experience the natural world — at least our four acres of it — as much as they need to. I've mentioned Marcia's needs: she rushes outdoors with passion and comes back replenished with tranquillity. Other children need this communion with the seasons, too, but they find it more casually.

I'm often asked if the children don't exploit the freedom to go outside when they want to. "If I let my class go out whenever they wanted to, they'd be out playing all the time!" a visiting teacher said, the tone of her voice implying as much criticism as the statement itself. I can't accept playing outside and learning inside as mutually exclusive. The examples I've given of outdoor behavior should suggest that there's a lot of learning going on. For those who want something more cognitive, I can mention Ricky's story about grasshoppers, dictated to Carrie and read aloud to the school at the meeting in the Forum just before the end of the school day. He'd been chasing grasshoppers for three days last September in the high grass at the back of the meadow. He'd caught a number of them, examined them carefully, let them go. He'd worked out for himself a way of telling grasshoppers from crickets. (I may add that he did this completely on his own.) He was telling Carrie about it when she asked him if he'd like her to write it down for him.

Because we understand the outdoors to be part of the school, not an escape from it, we're concerned with and alert to what the children are doing outside. Out of the concern comes a lot of talk with the children. On my part it tends to be about flowers and birds, falling leaves, how the snow drifts, the tracks of small animals, the way dry grasses stick up through the glazed snow this nearly-spring season. Shirley talks less and moves more — she runs with the children, and their running becomes a swooping, circling, tumbling, leaping dance. Or she becomes the leader in a most wonderful and inventive follow-the-leader.

If a child's spending a great deal of time outdoors, it's because he needs to. Observing him with care, we can often guess why. Then we can communicate this to him — let him know we know, and that we care. Earlier this fall Jerry had been walking by himself around the boundaries of our land, sometimes picking up a stone to look at, then dropping it. A number of children approached him at various times. The boys he accepted: he stopped, talked, squatted down to dig in the earth with one; with another, he ran up to the top of the sandpile. But he rejected the girls completely, turning his back on one, running away from another, yelling, "NO GIRLS!" at the third.

One day when we were standing side by side after such an incident, I said, "You sure have girl troubles."

"Stinky girls," he said.

He has an older sister and a younger one, which makes him the meat in the sandwich. Letting him know I knew about this seemed to help; at any rate, Jerry seemed more at ease with the girls as soon as he knew I "knew." However, a male visitor who was reading to a small group of which Jerry was the only male member reported that Jerry pushed Monica out of the way to sit next to him where he could see the pictures, and said, "No girls allowed." But having said it a couple of times, he paid no further attention to the fact that Monica and Kathy were sitting at the other side of the reader, and talked with them later about the story. He's been outdoors less often since we talked about his being out (the weather may account for this, of course) and less alone when he is out.

Janie is another case in point. She was hanging by her knees on the swing-set trapeze when her parents came to visit one day. They were distressed. "Why aren't you indoors?" her mother asked.

"I'd rather be out here," said Janie, upside down.

Mr. Wilder put it to me immediately: "We sent Jane here so she could put her good mind to work and not be held up by slower children. Why isn't she in here working?"

"She's learning in her own way," I answered. "She's been working hard all morning. Isn't it nice that she feels free enough to go out and swing some of the tension away?"

"What's she got to be tense about?" he asked aggressively.

I had some definite notions about that, notions which were getting stronger every minute. But I said, "Let's talk about it and see if we can find out."

Mrs. Wilder took an anxious look out the window. Janie was swinging high. "I wish she wouldn't play so hard," she said, and followed her husband and me into our conference space behind the one-way vision screen.

It wasn't a very productive meeting. The important thing to Mr. Wilder was how well his daughter was doing in arithmetic. I tried to say something about our structural approach to mathematics and how it helps children discover principles, but he wasn't really listening. When I told him Janie was doing very well indeed, he was pleased; when I suggested that the doggedness with which she went at it might have something to do with why she needed to go out and swing herself up to the sky, he wasn't interested. And when I tried to talk about her rigid perfectionism, he took it as a compliment, as I should have realized he would.

"She's getting that lovely dress dirty," was Mrs. Wilder's parting comment. At that point I was ready to scream at her that I'd asked parents to send their children to school in blue jeans. But a school director mustn't scream, even at adults.

Janie's use of the outdoors seems to me enormously important. Part of the perfectionism of the Wilder home is a drive towards achievement. One outcome of that was her mother's sending away for a kit of materials called "Teach Your Baby to Read" when Janie was two; and this resulted in her being drilled day after day on reading just a few months after her similarly insistent toilet training. "She worked at it very dutifully," her father says, and I'm for a moment not sure whether he's talking about the reading or the toilet training. Janie seems confused by it, too: working to learn something and working to produce a regular bowel movement are for her, if not the same thing, at least aspects of the same mode of relating to her parents. Going outdoors is a way of escaping from the demand, the insistence that she produce.

The importance of outdoors for Janie goes beyond the chance to swing or run or spin herself around in the whirligig. Last spring she sat for many minutes just watching a narcissus moving a little in the breeze. She feels the bark of trees, picks up handful after handful of snow to examine. A month ago she took me by the hand, led me outdoors to a patch of snow under one of the old apple trees, and pointed at the sprinkling of black dust on the frozen crust. I didn't know what she was pointing at. "They're alive!" she whispered. I bent down with her, and saw she was right — the black specks were tiny insects, jumping a fraction of an inch or wiggling a little on the snow.

Did I say I hoped our children would approach the world as researchers?

She finds in the outdoors, it seems to me, an order of a kind very different from that which she rigidly tries to create in school as a reflection of pressures at home. It's wishful thinking, of course — so many years to go, so much experience of school and home — but I keep hoping she will come to use her perfectionism in a way moderated by her quiet and loving relationship to natural things, and perhaps in their service.

Do they exploit the freedom to go outdoors? I hope so — exploit it for their own needs as Janie has learned to do. And that's the real point of her story. It's important that she can work off the tensions she lives with; it's wonderful that she may be able to find in the natural world an order which would give point and meaning to her precision; but the most important learning she's done in relation to the outdoors is that she has the freedom to make use of it when she needs and wants to. It's freedom I'm concerned with. One has to feel free in order to be confident. No person who isn't free is ever truly responsible. The only way I know how to teach freedom is to make it a basic factor in the lives of the people being taught.

I was timid about making the outdoors free to the children when I first started the school. Like the visiting teacher who was so critical of our freedom, I was afraid the children would never do any "schoolwork" if they had the option of going outdoors. So I kept them inside the first half of every morning. Then at about ten thirty I'd put a green sign on the door as a signal to the children that they could go out if they wanted to. This came to mean to some children that school was over for the day — drop what you're doing and scramble out into the yard. Those who weren't anxious to go out, finding themselves alone, would often stop what they were doing and, more or less reluctantly, join the others. School was becoming more and more a half-morning operation.

It's interesting to me that my first inclination then was

to cut down the outdoors time, perhaps to the half hour just before the end of school. (I find it hard to recapture the person I was then — how alien a response that seems now!) But I didn't cut the time down, because I saw how important it was to some of the children to be outdoors. It was more than a year, however, before I was ready to take that leap of faith in the children which made it possible for me to rethink the whole matter of in and out, work and play, living and learning, and my commitment to children's needs as children experience them.

The rethinking continues. I ask myself if my fascination with the Montessori and Leicestershire materials makes me communicate to the children an expectation that they will spend the major amount of their time at school indoors at work with those materials — and thus, that the freedom I tell them they have is, in some unspoken, intangible way, limited. Could I truly accept the decision of a four-year-old to spend all or almost all of his school time outdoors? I have to work this kind of thing out for myself, as honestly as I can, so that I can be honest with the children and their parents.

There are two other kinds of freedom which parents are sometimes anxious about. One is the simple freedom of food: there are crackers and juice out all the time, and a child who wants something to eat can go and get it, as Jan did after he'd spelled out his father's name. The other is a child's freedom of being able to move from one kind of learning activity to another as he wishes to.

I don't know why these two freedoms should be so distressing. Both of them are part of adult life. Sitting here in front of my fireplace tonight, scribbling on a yellow pad, I've gotten hungry and thirsty. I got up once to get some bread and cheese, again to dig a half-empty quart of ginger ale out of the back of the refrigerator, a third time to fetch an apple. You've probably done something of the same kind while reading what I've been writing, and we all do when we're watching television. If it's all right for you and me to get snacks when we want them, why is it

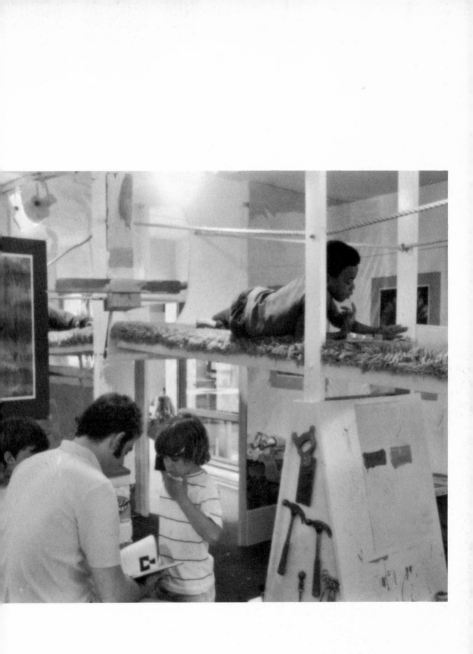

looked upon so suspiciously when children do it? "They have to learn that they can't have everything they want when they want it," answers a nursery-school teacher, and I am reminded of the many similar statements which led me to start my own school.

Substitute the verb "do" for "have," and the criticism goes for the second kind of freedom — the implication is that children mustn't be allowed to do what they want to because they have to learn that the world is full of frustrations. But they've learned that long before coming to the Early Learning Center, and they're learning it every day, and will be for the rest of their lives. We have something else to teach them — what is supposed to be the heart and soul of their culture, the freedom to choose and be and do, and the use of that freedom in making careful and conscious choices, in being and doing in the best way one can.

As eating something when you want to eat it is part of adult life, so is moving from one activity to another. When I'm seriously concerned about something, I work on it hard until it's finished. When it's one of a number of incidental things I want to do, I may very well work on one for a bit, then on another. Various drafts of material for this book, for instance, have been in my desk for a couple of years or more — things I worked on at odd moments. Now that the publisher has set a deadline and I have a coauthor, the writing is no longer an incidental activity.

I find just this kind of pattern with the children. It's not boredom or restlessness or lack of discipline that moves them from one part of the room to another, from one activity or piece of equipment to another. Rather, it's a matter of having done enough for the moment to satisfy one's need. Michael arranged the blocks of the Montessori brown stairs in order of ascending size, as he might have done with the red rods or any of their step-cousins, and that was that. He moved over to a game of concentration, watched for a few minutes, and then began playing. Children vary greatly in the needs they bring to different learning materials. Danny will work long and hard putting the right white tiles into the blue frame of the Leicestershire number ladders, but spend only a passing moment with the cutout letters. Alice, on the other hand, has only the briefest interest in the Montessori gold beads, and will abandon them immediately if she gets the message that there's some reading aloud going on.

("Gets the message." There's a kind of bush telegraph operating at the Early Learning Center. Children learn from activities other children are taking part in many feet away, as if by a kind of telepathy. I've seen Alice working with materials she's much involved with — cards with pictures and words on them, for instance — at the same time that Carrie's reading aloud a new story. Alice continues the work she's doing, apparently completely absorbed in it, but later on turns out to know the new story. Of this message-getting, more later.)

I must leave the children for a moment to say something about freedom as I understand it in relation to them. First, it seems to me there's a very important difference between freedom and laissez-faire. People are inextricably bound together in a network of mutual aid, caring, responsibility, cooperation. Freedom exists within this interaction as the liberty persons grant to each other out of their faith in and concern for each other. Such freedom is nourished by respect and appreciation; from it trust grows, and within it individuality flourishes.

I define what we have at the Early Learning Center as freedom because we grant it to the children and they grant it to each other in a setting in which people care very much for each other and are very observant of each other. Laissez-faire invokes for me such notions as neglect, disregard, lack of care, rejection. I have been in schools which are advertised as free and found harried teachers attempting to respond to the whims of bored children while others were running screaming through the classroom. I don't think anyone is truly free in such an atmosphere.

Carl Rogers, author of *Freedom to Learn,* is a psychologist famous for making freedom into a powerful therapeutic and educational tool. The key to his work with people is his own great strength, it seems to me. In watching him at work I have been impressed by how surely, quietly, attentively he is granting freedom to the person or persons he's working with. When someone cares enough about you to attend with intensity to what you're doing and respond to it acceptingly and uncritically, you find freedom in yourself. How totally different that is from turning your back on an individual and pretending that by so doing you have freed him!

Second, not only does freedom not exist in a vacuum, it cannot exist with emptiness at its center. We are preoccupied in the last third of the twentieth century with freedom *from* something or other — communism, fascism, immorality, prudery, lockstep education, segregation or integration, drug laws or drug users. But freedom *from* so often ends up denying freedom *for.*

I am concerned at the Early Learning Center that freedom should be *for* something. To turn a two-year-old "free" with paints, brushes, and paper is to confuse him, perhaps so frustrate him that he will not want to use paints for a long time to come. That is not freedom; it is the most irresponsible laissez-faire, masquerading under the name of "freedom from artificial restrictions and imposed standards." I am not out to restrict or impose. I am out to teach. I can show a child how to use a brush; later I may suggest that he try out three different ways of using brushes. I like to paint, and occasionally I lay out my materials and begin painting during school hours; usually several children come to watch and after a while they're painting beside me. I don't make a lesson out of it. Often nothing is said, but sometimes we talk about each other's paintings. I don't insist or require, but I realize I'm furnishing the children with a resource they are free to make use of.

At times we have had consultants who were quite exacting. A man came to teach Chinese calligraphy to those children who were interested. His enthusiasm and consummate skill reached them, and they received him each time with excitement. He made rigorous demands on the children — the brush must be held just so, the movement of arm and wrist must be of just such a nature — but they understood these demands as necessary and appropriate to the process he was teaching. They seemed to realize that such discipline was not an invasion of freedom; they freely chose to submit themselves to it for the satisfaction of learning a new skill.

Freedom at the Early Learning Center has content, because we are constantly at work preparing the environment. I want the children's freedom to lead them to things which are interesting and intriguing. Example: a sorting box — a box in which there are new objects every day or every several days, chosen to differ in one or two qualities, for the children to sort into categories or sets. One day it's buttons, all white pearl but of different sizes. Another day it's squares of colored plastic I've found on Canal Street, all the same size but of a rainbow of different colors. A third day it's empty spools. A fourth, it might be bottle tops. We're always on the lookout for materials.

Skills and concepts need extension, so part of the freedom is to move from graduated rods to graduated blocks, cubes, spheres. Or from the world of school materials to the practical world of measuring cups, nuts and bolts, safety pins, or (more puzzling, for the size can be changed) rubber bands, all of which come in various sizes and can be sorted from big to little. Or to carry the individual skill of balancing on a wooden rail into the group activity of follow-the-leader. We are constantly on the alert to give children interesting options, genuine choice among worthwhile alternatives. I think we are creating an environment in which freedom has meaning.

Finally, let me say that I don't believe much in abstractions. I've written a lot about freedom, and I talk about it a good deal, but that's just shorthand for some operations we carry out with children. I like to see children doing what interests them because they are learning, not because they are little symbols of freedom. When I tell a child that I want him to sit in a certain place or that I can't let him do what he's doing, I don't understand this as a compromise with freedom; I see it as a way of making a better learning situation for all the children, and I do it within what I know and the children know is a real respect for them as free human beings.

Freedom is a way of interacting. We desperately need to realize this. Freedom is an aspect of an interdependent society. It involves discipline, skill, conscience, a far-reaching awareness of consequences — in short, responsibility. Like any way of dealing with the world, freedom has to be lived to be learned. We are trying to help children learn it by living it.

Does this disquisition add to your image of the school? It should at least make clear that the Early Learning Center is not a place where children bumble from indulgence to indulgence, followed by anxious teachers desperately trying to cope with fifty different demands. Rather — as much as we can make it so — it's a place where children are at work on tasks important to them, of such a nature as to convey messages about the world of things and processes, of problems and ways of working on problems, which exists outside the place and time that are the school. As such, the Early Learning Center is the best kind of real world we can make it.

Five

A Crime
Without a Name

"It's a middle-class sort of school, isn't it?"

I'd been telling a new friend about the Early Learning Center and showing her some of the pictures the people at the Educational Facilities Laboratory took when they were assembling material for the film. Once I thought I knew what the term meant. Today it's lost its specificity and become vilification. To be middle-class is to be guilty of a crime without a name.

My first impulse was to say no, no, twenty percent of our

children are from ghetto families. But that would be to admit the validity of the implicit condemnation. Instead, I told her about individual children and what I think they have in common, from whatever backgrounds they come. But the "middle-class" label still rankles.

"Of course, you can do those things in a private school — you're dealing with a better class of children" is one teacher's excuse for the rigid rules and stereotyped curriculum every child must follow in a new classroom.

A Head Start teacher, earnestly reinforcing her pupils with a pat on the knee or an invented show of happy surprise when they answer "Block!" to her question, "What's this I'm holding in my hand?" implies that I've got an easy job because I'm teaching bright children from well-to-do backgrounds.

And then there's the preschool expert who looks at our building and says, "It's almost too lovely!" and tells me I should hang up the children's paintings rather than the Marimekko fabrics, leave things a little disarranged, "make it look like a place children play in." In short, beauty and orderliness are antithetical to learning, and if I weren't hung up on middle-class values I'd recognize that real education happens only when there is chaos.

I'm sorry.

Not about the school or about orderliness and beauty. I'm sorry about the kind of thinking which leads to criticisms of this kind. I'm sorry about the failure of these critics to study children and compare their findings with those of others — Maria Montessori, John Dewey, Catherine Stern, Sylvia Ashton-Warner, Edward Yeomans, John Holt and many, many others.

Three notes and then some elaboration.

Note One: the backgrounds of the children. Of about fifty-five children, ten are from families in the hard-core poverty group with incomes below $3,000 a year, living in Stamford's low-income housing project. The children are on full scholarship. About ten more are from families with incomes in the

$7,000-to-$12,000 range. Sending their children to the school requires tight budgeting. There is a middle group, some twenty children, whose parents probably make about $15,000 to $18,-000, a comfortable but in no sense high income for this community. Another dozen are from the next bracket up, families with incomes which may go as high as $25,000. Finally, there are two children from what I'd call rich families.

We're missing children from one group — families above the level of desperate poverty but not far enough above it to be able to pay our $800-a-year tuition. Since such persons comprise a substantial part of the city's population, our group is somewhat skewed towards the high end of the income curve by comparison with all of Stamford, but less so than any other independent private school population I know of — and less than all but a few of the public schools (because the public schools are established on neighborhood or district lines, which are to an extent economic lines).

Note Two: a better class of children. I don't know whether we're working with "bright" children or not; brightness isn't a characteristic we try to measure or a criterion for admitting children to the school. The interest of parents in this kind of education is a criterion, whether the parents live in the low-income housing project or on a ten-acre estate. This means that the children come from homes where someone cares about education. To the extent that this affects the children, we may indeed have a better class of children than would be found in the worst public schools. It may be useful to remember, however, that the methods and materials we use were developed for ghetto or working-class schools, where they proved enormously successful.

Note Three: order and chaos. Chaos happens when schools are poorly equipped, when teachers attempt to respond to children's whims rather than furnishing the children with many interesting options in choice of learning materials, and when reward and punishment, praise and condemnation (actual or implicit) are used to control or manipulate children. The chaos becomes confused with learning only when these characteristics occur within a situation which also happens to have enough freedom in it so that children learn in spite of the chaos. They would learn more if the freedom were less compromised by disorder.

Children like the quiet, orderly beauty of the school. I think they like the posters and prints I hang. I have put up some of their paintings which I think of as good art — but I know that by and large they don't want their work displayed; the learning — and it is joyful and important to learn about pattern and color, the wonder of the accidental and the pleasure of the controlled, most of all about the discovery that one can make things happen — the learning resides in the doing, not in the product. As we grow older, becoming more the creatures of our culture, we forget this, for in our adult sophistication a process is incomplete without, and is distilled into, a product. For the child, the painting — finished or abandoned — is no such object of virtue. How surprised I was to find that a great many children didn't recognize their own paintings the day after they made them.

To the charge of maintaining an orderly house I plead guilty.

To the charge of irrelevance-through-middle-classness I plead not guilty.

The work of George Dennison at the First Street School, as he reports it in *The Lives of Children,* moves me deeply; it is infuriating that there should be no funds to continue such an experiment. I am indignant at the ghetto school situations Jonathan Kozol describes in *Death at an Early Age.* I am heartened by what Sylvia Ashton-Warner has been able to do in New Zealand with Maori children. It's encouraging to remember that Maria Montessori's work in education started as part of an overall attack on the dreadful conditions she found in the slums of Italian cities.

The work we do at the Early Learning Center is intimately related — in aim, in method, in materials used, in fundamental assumptions about how children learn and what and why — to these persons and their efforts. That our school includes not only poor children but rich children and many children in between must not be thought of as invalidating its program. Our emphasis, on helping children learn concepts and construct meanings, is identical with that in some of the best Head Start centers. I think we do it better than many of the centers do because we've thought more about learning materials and about the uses of freedom.

Our approach is totally removed from an approach being used in some other child-care centers — and used increasingly because it takes little equipment and little training, and produces immediate results. That approach is, fundamentally, operant conditioning, or a bastardization of it: a child is rewarded (a pat on the hand, a smile, praise, a bit of candy) for saying the "right" word when some stimulus is given. Vocabulary is learned quickly this way, but learned superficially and outside the context of the life of any individual child; it is therefore neither long-lasting nor of any particular use to the child in enriching his experience and developing in him that ability to deal with the world which we call intelligence.

One of my dreams — more than that; I've worked hard on it but as yet without results — is that we can have a number of schools like the Early Learning Center set up here and there, to demonstrate our approach, help more teachers learn our ways of working with children, and show that what we do doesn't depend for its success on working with "a better class of children."

I've always thought of my school as a prototype. That's one reason for this book: to urge others to start schools in which our way of working is adapted to other communities and to the personalities of other teachers. But specifically I want to see a school very much like this one in architecture, equipment, and approach started in one of Stamford's low-income areas. I think we could do wonders for children many teachers call ineducable.

I'm asked sometimes how many children we turn down at the Early Learning Center. The answer is none. I'm reasonably sure that what we do at ELC is good education for *any* child. We do turn down some families, though. Education is always a joint venture. Teachers, parents, and the child are all intimately involved in it. Friends and relations play a part. Indirectly, the child's whole environment is learning material. But his family is his most important educational resource.

Donald's mother called up to say she wanted to register him in the school. I told her I made a point of visiting children and their families to talk about the school; might I call on them? She seemed a little surprised but said yes, of course, she understood — could I come Saturday morning? I could.

The house was one of the largest in an expensive part of town, a Victorian mansion renovated and redecorated with great attention to style. I rang the doorbell and was admitted by a maid in uniform. At the right of the hall were two living rooms, beautifully furnished. I was shown into neither. Instead, the maid took me into a little room on the left which might at one time have been a closet.

Mother was aggressively intellectual, eager to show her knowledge of Montessori (which was shallow and at times incorrect). I was informed that Donald's two older sisters were at the country day school nearby — informed in a manner which at one sweep eliminated any and all differences between private schools, as long as they were private. Father was wearing the Ivy League disguise. He treated me a bit like Avon Calling. A lot of his questions were about cost.

Donald was brought in by the maid after ten minutes of general conversation. He was dressed for the occasion — shirt, tie, and jacket, all three-year-old sizes. He was ordered to shake hands. After sitting on the edge of a stool for a while, he began to act his age — move about the room, make a little noise — and was told by his father to keep quiet.

After a while I said thank you and went away from there. A few days later I wrote them a brief note saying I was sorry, we were trying to balance the school group by ages and sexes and we simply didn't have a place for Donald. It was a white lie: we do try to balance the group, but we could have made room for Donald if we thought there was a ghost of a chance of working things out with his parents. I didn't think there was. Donald would have come to school every day from a way of life so inconsistent with the school's methods and attitudes that he would have lived in constant confusion. His parents were not interested in the school as a place for learning, only as a place to put Donald.

Do my criteria begin to come clear? I think we need — though we don't always find — parents who understand what we're doing and are in general agreement with it; who are ready to work with us in the joint venture of education. (May I say in passing that the parents of the scholarship children from the housing project meet these criteria in a most rewarding way? Certainly that's one big reason their children have worked out so well in the school.)

Many good things happen in home visits. I see a coat closet with pegs set a yard from the floor so children can hang up their clothes. I see houses lived in by children, not marked off with forbidden areas. I see a lot of affectionate byplay between parents and their children.

Paul and his mother and I had a three-way conversation; when his father came in, it was four-way. For a while it adjourned to Paul's room upstairs, because he wanted to show me his toys — which were kept on wide, low shelves, not all heaped in a box or thrown in a corner. A good visit all around, I thought. I was reassured, not threatened, by the fact that Paul's father seemed to be feeding the results of our conversation into a shrewd data-processing kind of mind: because of the kind of person he'd shown himself to be, I knew he'd be using that mind to help the school. (He has been.) For what it's worth, Paul's family is among the ten or so in the $7,000-to-$12,000 range, at the lower end of it, I should guess. With a few important exceptions, those who contribute most to the school in time and energy are from this group.

What goes on at home is of great importance to a school like ours. Education is a matter of making sense out of experience, and the biggest part of the experience is at home. Ann Louise has to make some personal sense of the exurbanite culture with its free-flowing tensions; Adam has to make sense of poverty and blackness; Janie has to make sense of an overemphasis on perfection. Parent conferences are tremendously useful — even such frustrating occasions as the conference I described with Janie's parents, I tell myself. I can see the school lives of the children in a larger context. And sometimes I find out fascinating things about the school and how children learn in it.

Sasha was born to parents who married late. The children of their friends are already grown, and Sasha lives at home in an adult society. His parents are aware of the limits this imposes on him and happy to have him use the school mainly as a social center. As I've suggested earlier, he's not the only child for whom we serve that purpose — modern urban and exurban life doesn't provide much natural social life for children.

For his first half year in school, Sasha was mainly a watcher, not unhappy but not much involved. He was one of the youngest children, and we were willing to wait. Then he became part of one of those small groups children of three or four often make — pairs or trios; he and Maria and Jerry did everything together (he was the brains, Maria was the boss, Jerry was the follower). At five, he was part of a gang. Reacting like Ann Louise to an age when ambition far outstrips ability or patience, he and a few other children would move somewhat randomly, sometimes raucously, through the school. We would remind them that there were others in the world, and they were rarely a problem. But like many five-year-olds, they seemed to have given up conceptual learning for the time being.

One day Peter brought the six-to-nines into the building, as he does from time to time. He was teaching them math with the Cuisenaire rods (smaller than Montessori's red rods but developed from them and from Catherine Stern's similar materials). Sasha and his gang of three or four dashed through, en route from the gym set to the great outdoors, stopping to wave to Peter and a couple of his boys who'd been in the younger group the year before. I reminded them it would be clean-up time soon, and out they went.

The next week, in a conference with Sasha's parents, I discovered that Sasha had talked to them with great excitement about the Cuisenaire rods and demonstrated a real knowledge of what it was Peter was teaching. Was it just that the rods intrigued him, I asked. No, much more than that — he'd learned what the rods were being used to teach.

How? I've spoken before of the way children in one part of the room seem to apprehend what's going on elsewhere in the school. I've read Lawrence Kubie and Richard Jones on the wonderful capacity of the human nervous system to absorb and retain what's going on in the environment. But I've rarely had such documentation of the instantaneous and effortless nature of real learning; nor could I have had it without regular contact with Sasha's parents.

Incidents like this suggest to me how haphazard much learning is. It comes out of living fully in a rich environment. It comes from trying to make sense — order, pattern, meaning — out of a lot of things; but it doesn't come in an orderly way. (Or let's say, rather, that the orderliness is hidden deep within each child.)

My final elaboration must be on learning, that process of exploring the environment to make sense out of it. The first learning we see is like Danny's: when he scrubs tables or puts blocks in rows — he needs to make things right. Two-year-olds put things in piles, scrub, pick up crumbs one at a time, tell their parents to hang up their hats and coats, want the doors all closed or all open. At the same time they are doing some elementary exploring of cause and effect — what happens when you drop things or throw things or pour things. Towers sometimes are built just to be knocked down. Danny's first use of the Unifix cubes was to dump them out on the rug all at once and then plop them back, cube by cube.

Many schools start such children with art by giving them finger paints or water paints, brushes, paper. We've found that they mainly want to mess about with colors. Shirley has answered this need by mixing up various kinds of liquids — water with vegetable dyes, thick cornstarch paste in several colors, and an assortment of textures and viscosities between those extremes. They're mix-and-mess materials: see what will happen when you pour blue into yellow or when you stir something thick and sticky into something watery.

Exploring becomes more wide-ranging as the children grow. It turns to questions of magnitude or extent. Danny needed to build the Unifix cube train all the way across the school; at another time, he had to make a construction which would use all the cubes. Sasha's trio — three-year-olds — went through a period when they had to collect together all of the household materials they could move and set them up in the Wendy House; for an hour or so there would be a scurrying back and forth to bring in object after object.

The collecting involves classifying, which is the beginning of a certain kind of rational abstract thinking, the kind we call logic. Our theory of instruction is, most simply, to help a child develop as far and as fully as he can at each stage of growth he goes through, so at this point we make sure he knows the various learning materials through which he can work on classifying things. Ann Louise plunged into these materials with enormous zest — into them and out the other side, as if for her this stage of development was to be raced through at an exhausting pace.

Artwork at this point is the making of collections on paper. One child sets himself the task of covering every bit of the paper with poster paint or crayon. Another wants to use every color possible. I suggest to them the collage: we cut out figures from advertisements, bits of cloth or yarn, scraps of colored paper, and paste them down to make a fantastic and fascinating collection.

We explore, too, the enormous variety of sense experiences open to a child. Let me remind you of Shirley's work again: she mixes up things to feel — the dryness of breadcrumbs and cornflakes; the soft, almost slippery feeling of rolled oats; the various ways macaroni can feel: dry from the package, cooked to a tough *al dente,* or boiled to that sticky, slimy snakiness to slither through the fingers. She has a big assortment of sound makers: bells and whistles, drums and blocks and xylophones. She can put all sorts of flavors on crackers or in gelatin. There are spices and perfumes, wood shavings, rose leaves, peanut butter and lubricating oil to smell and identify.

And each of these collections of sense experiences can be classified, sorted and categorized by various criteria.

This period seems to be followed by one in which children put the emphasis on controlling things and making things. The things made may be objects or the outcomes of processes. In neither case are they made with any sense that they are to be kept — the important thing is to show that something can be done. The grading and sorting of the Montessori color tablets is an activity with such an end in view. Building words with cutout letters, putting together a jigsaw map of the world, using clay to shape an object: in such activities a child controls materials towards a desired end. Alice's painting and woodworking are good examples. Her painting is more sophisticated than it used to be because she's now using processes to create a painting rather than just to have fun with the process. She's learned simple woodworking techniques in order to make something, not just because the techniques themselves are interesting.

It's at this point, of course, that many of the children learn to read. Much arithmetic is learned, too — not so much as numbers to be manipulated on paper but as a knowledgeable use of rods, blocks, beads, balances. Thus, Michael's quiet confidence about the solid square of Unifix cubes — sixteen of them, four to a side.

Then we come to the difficult time — five and a half for many children — when all of this learning creates needs and ambitions young children don't have the knowledge, the coordination, the strength, or the patience to implement; and when it first becomes clear to them that they are essentially their own masters. The partial resolution Ann Louise has made — helping the younger children, sometimes teaching them — is one of the better ways we know of to deal with this problem; I must point out that it is possible only in an ungraded, mixed-age schoolroom, and that its success depends on the older child's perceiving that she is really needed and useful.

I don't mean to imply that learning stops at this point. It does become complicated — in good part, I think, because a shift is taking place. Let me call what's been going on thus far simple learning or primary learning — how to carry out this or that process or, in its later stages, how to achieve this or that effect. Now a child wants to put all of these things together to serve some large end, and a whole new phase of learning has to begin — call it complex learning or secondary learning. The transition from simple to complex is a difficult one for many children. Tasks are very frustrating: what appears easy and straightforward as the child contemplates it becomes impossible or nearly so as it is attempted, because it calls for information and skills the child doesn't have or a kind of planning he's not able to do.

Ann Louise's helping with the younger children is a long step towards this more complex behavior. The job is an immediate one — something that has to be done now. It's immediately evident *what* has to be done — help a child with outdoor clothing, read a book, show someone the little bells to be arranged in ascending pitch. It's a good introduction to secondary learning because it asks Ann Louise to put to use, in the context of real need a lot of the things she knows. Janie's interest in nature could involve her in this kind of complex learning, too — there are books to read, things to collect and classify, drawings or paintings to make, stories to be written. We can help her make use of an interest of this kind, but the interest itself is something she had to discover for herself.

As far as I can tell, children from all sorts of backgrounds follow this sequence as they learn. Each does it differently, each chooses his own activities and materials to learn with and through. But the movement and the stages the child goes through seem to be universal, at least within this reasonably broad spectrum of American children. If you were to visit the school, I think you would not be able to tell our scholarship students from the others. I don't think of any of them as belonging to any social or economic class. I do think of all of them very much as belonging to the school. Like many good schools, the Early Learning Center is a kind of classless society. People are doing what they are interested in doing to learn what they are ready to learn. We are helping them as much as we can.

Six

Beginnings

Stamford, Connecticut, in the fall of 1963. A thirty-year-old housewife with a two-and-a-half-year-old child drives purposefully from one nursery school to another. Why is it always the same old blocks, dirty from years of handling, the same old dolls, the same easels splotched with poster paint? Why do the teachers look so tired and the children so hectic — or the teachers so frantic and the children so bored? Is this just New England getting grimly ready for its five-month winter?

We stop at Muzzio's Boatyard to watch the men hauling forty-foot cruisers up the ways for the winter. David asks bright questions and points out to me things I hadn't noticed — the black and yellow Halloween Yacht Club flag on many of these little boats; the hairy seaweed below the waterline of a small sloop recently hauled, standing in its cradle. What could any of those schools we visited do for this questioning, sensitive, alert child as he tries to understand the world around him?

Behind us lies the city, one hundred thousand people more or less, half the size of my native Richmond and half a world away, it seems: Yankee sharpness and Italian volubility so very different from the softer, slower speech and movement of Virginia, the crisp New England fall chilly in the air at night, still a surprise even though it's been a decade (adventuresome years? wasted years?) since I left home. In spite of art school in New York, and Altman's, where I was an assistant buyer, and managing stores in Florida and on the West Coast for Alexander Shields, and marrying an advertising man, and having David, and organizing a Sunday School . . . still I feel surprise at fall, and a sense of being amid alien corn. Why? The boredom of the exurbanite wife, perhaps. Some failure of identity: who am I, after all? What have I done that's worth anything? What do I know, what can I do?

And is there a way of helping my little Davy and the child who will soon follow him towards a better relation with his world? (Better — with greater meaning, a sense of adequacy based in real competence. And may they never suffer boredom or that suspicion that ten years of living have been thrown away.)

We walked through the waterfront neighborhood with its strange mixture of the mercantile nineteenth century — a ship chandler's store redolent of creosote, an outside stairway with a small sign indicating it leads to a sail loft — and the affluent twentieth century — restaurants for the yacht-club set, garages for their cars, boatyards full of polished mahogany and shining brass. We passed a century-old house, unpainted for at least the last quarter of its life. In a dusty window was a hand-printed sign, CLAIRVOYANT. I thought it would be fun to come back sometime and see what I could find out. The future seemed at the moment full of trivia: dentists and doctors, the decorator about new curtains, the duty dinners to give and go to. At heart I knew it was empty — all that I could look forward to with any intellectual interest was the research I did every week for an adult Bible class I was teaching at the Episcopal church.

What would I have said if the clairvoyant had told me that in 1970 I would be a consultant to a state department of education wanting advice on centers for preschool children? That my name would one day be on a book about something I'd done important enough to write a book about? "Fascinating," I would have said, "but that's not me. I gave up my interest in teaching ten years ago, I'm not a writer, and the biggest project I've ever started was a men's fashion show." The seer would have been on surer ground predicting Christopher's birth — something of a foregone conclusion, with a fifty percent chance of being right about the sex. And had she spoken of divorce, I would have admitted the possibility, but only because it seemed so common among the people we knew — life in an exurbanite community isn't conducive to the best in family relations.

But I didn't consult her that day or any other. By the time curiosity did lead me to a clairvoyant — a white-haired Vermont housewife with an apron tied across her middle, sitting in an old rocking chair in her farmhouse living room while her husband was out milking the cows — enough had happened in my life so that I was ready to consider any and all eventualities.

What David and I were looking for in the fall of 1963 wasn't, I realized, unrelated to the future, though I was examining very present situations. Going to school is one of the big steps a child takes into tomorrow, at two or four or six. But what it means for tomorrow is vitally tied to what happens today. Is the step taken happily and confidently? Is it into a place and time rich in the possibilities for experience and the possibilites for dealing with experience?

In 1963 I put the question in much simpler terms. Going into a room full of silent and solemn children, painted in nursery pink and baby blue with frilly white curtains at the few high windows, talking to the large, rather shapeless woman whose peasant blouse and sugar-sweet voice seemed to be one with the decor, I was asking myself, "What will David learn here?"

I wasn't sure what I wanted him to learn. I did know it had a lot to do with his quick, alert perceptions of the world, and the quest behind his questions — every child's quest for meaning and understanding. There had been so much to understand during his very new life: missiles in Cuba, a confusing war in Algeria, men being shot into the sky at the tops of rockets to circle the earth for hours. But just as important to him were the leaves changing color on the trees, the boats being railroaded out of the water, the older children in the neighborhood going off each morning, in noisy groups, to be away until midafternoon, leaving the world of streets and stores to women and babies.

To use a term from philosophy which since 1963 has come to mean much to me, I wanted him to learn about his being-in-the-world: who he was, what he could do, what he needed to know, and how he could find it out. In short, I wanted him to learn what it seemed to me at thirty I had never learned — how to be a whole person whose actions and decisions weren't determined by haphazard fragments of experience, unrelated memory traces, borrowed opinions, barely recognized prejudices.

Mrs. Mandible's blue and white nursery wouldn't do it, I was quite sure — the experiences available to children were so limited, so surely planned to reinforce her view of the child's world as sweet, cute, full of pastel colors and baby animals as portrayed in cheap children's books.

Nor would the parents' cooperative school I visited, where a

dozen children were pulling each other's hair while three mothers gossiped over coffee in the kitchen and a sixteen-year-old high-school dropout tried to maintain order.

Nor that baby academy where the children sat in rows to be drilled in vocabulary, modeled with clay side by side at a crowded table under the instruction of a loud-voiced woman in a smock, and came back from a ten-minute recess to string beads — ten white ones, then a blue one, ten more white ones, then a red one.

Nor the play school — all baby carriages and dolls and dress-up clothes and tricycles and blocks, and God forbid any child should want to learn to read: "Childhood's so brief and precious a time, we wouldn't want to spoil it, would we? And their little eyes aren't really ready for letters yet."

Sentimentality, a failure to respect the needs of children, lack of planning, rigidity — I knew they were the wrong approaches to teaching young children, and I had a dim idea of why they were wrong.

After high school I'd spent two years at a junior college in Virginia taking a course supposed to prepare one for teaching. I'd dropped it, in large part because the work had been so frightfully dull, but also because I had realized we were dealing hardly at all with how children learn and teachers teach, but almost entirely with what gets called "classroom management," a euphemism for various forms of repressive or punitive discipline. Just as it had been in that teaching curriculum, the major problem in these nursery schools around Stamford seemed to be how to keep order. Treating the children like babies was one response. Handing them to a baby-sitter was another. Drilling and grilling was a third. Running an indoor playground a fourth. There were others, equally disappointing.

Then someone mentioned a Montessori school in a nearby town.

Montessori was in my mind.

I'd been sitting in a waiting room (doctor? dentist? beauty

parlor?) turning over the pages of a magazine when I'd come on an article about Dr. Omar Khayyam Moore and his talking typewriter — an electronic gadget which responded to a child's pressing a key by telling him the name of the letter on the key, or asked him to spell a word and then locked all but the right keys. The article spoke of Maria Montessori's belief that children were eager to read, just as they were eager to find or make order in the world around them, and that reading was simply the application of skills ready to evolve or unfold in every child.

I was intrigued. I'd been a little involved in Stamford politics and knew how concerned some of the school people were about children from impoverished backgrounds who never seemed to catch up with their more fortunate schoolmates — in reading or in anything else. I sent for a film about the talking typewriter and showed it to school people and a few church groups, but there wasn't money for so complex and expensive a gadget.

The Montessori notion about the inborn potential for skills which would unfold, given the right situation at the right time, stuck with me. The name kept turning up. There seemed to be a Montessori revival going on: magazine and newspaper articles described children busy with blocks of various kinds, each child doing a particular task, his equipment on a small mat. Other children were shining shoes or scrubbing small square cloths on old-fashioned washboards. Nothing was said about classroom management — apparently all of the children were too busy to need to be kept in order. So it was with real interest I went to visit the Montessori school an hour's drive away.

I was told that I couldn't watch the school at work, though I could come to a demonstration hour — the children mustn't be disturbed by casual onlookers while they were busy learning, teaching themselves. The demonstration was interesting. The children seemed to know what they were doing, and were doing it with little direction from teachers. A lesson with the sand-paper letters — a child tracing letters with his forefinger, sounding each one as he felt its shape both as texture and as the muscular pattern in which he moved his hand and arm — made great sense to me.

So David became a Montessori pupil, and I became a Montessori mother.

Like the elephant's child, I have an insatiable curiosity. So I asked David's teacher a lot of questions. For the first time I was getting answers that fitted together into a clear and consistent view of how children learn and how a school can help them learn. Now I know that I was learning a philosophy of education, and I've been able to go on from that beginning to a larger and more satisfactory framework — modifying these early questions and answers by my firm belief in the freedom of the child to be and do, explore and try out, and work towards his own style of learning and living.

I wasn't thinking about those larger questions then. The wonderful inventiveness of the Montessori materials, each designed to help a child discover and practice a particular way of thinking, fascinated me. It was equally fascinating to conceive of complex skills — or at least the potential for developing those skills — as somehow built into children. If this was true, a child didn't need to be instructed: he just needed to be given a situation in which he could practice what was waiting to be practiced.

Because I enjoyed talking about these things with the teacher, she enjoyed talking about them with me. Soon there came that critical day when she asked me if I'd ever thought of becoming a Montessori teacher.

I never had — not consciously, anyway. But from that moment, it was as if I'd been thinking about it all my life — there was no question in my mind; it simply had to be.

I would get the training.

I might even start my own school.

Seven

Preparation

Five days a week from nine to five, eight weeks of the summer of 1964, I spent at Fairleigh Dickinson University taking the Montessori training course. I'd had to get all sorts of testimony to be admitted — letters from Montessori teachers and people I'd worked with in various citizen groups in Stamford, telephone calls from friends. For the training program is on the graduate level, and I had only those few semesters of junior college behind me, far behind.

A friend and I commuted from Stamford, an hour-and-a-half drive across the southern tip of Connecticut, a bit of Westchester County in New York, the Hudson River, and some of New Jersey. Fortunately the driving was out of the commuter traffic pattern: going one way I would sail past the bumper-to-bumper traffic headed into New York; going the other I'd meet the haggard homecomers.

There were two graduate courses, one in child development, one in child psychology, presented completely through lectures. In the psychology course there were exams every week — just as in high school, multiple-choice questions for which we had to memorize things like Piaget's eight sensori-motor stages. We would stop halfway along the road each morning and drill each other. But Nancy Rambusch's course — child development — was exciting. She was so full of information, so dynamic as she paced back and forth on the little stage talking to the forty-five of us. She knew better than to give us multiple-choice exams; instead, she asked each of us to invent a piece of equipment.

Some afternoons we could go — in groups of ten, for periods of forty minutes — to watch the demonstration Montessori class. It was taught by one of those whispering teachers, and all the children whispered too, out of respect for the miracle of learning, perhaps, or in deference to the late great Maria Montessori. We sat behind a rail, on which was posted this instruction: IF A CHILD LOOKS AT YOU, DROP YOUR EYES. I guess we dutifully did. Attention was supposed to be on the materials, not on human beings, or at least not on us.

Other afternoons we'd practice instructing each other with the materials. This can be fun if you don't have to take it too seriously. But when a group of full-grown women solemnly present to each other the cylinders, or tell each other — in the precisely learned phrases of the master teacher, with the exact prescribed gestures, the properly modulated voice — how to scrub a table, all sixteen steps, it's nothing short of ridiculous, a scene from the theater of the absurd!

Once a week we had a seminar. From time to time — not often enough, I thought — there were outside speakers. So went the summer.

At the end of it we were examined. Three master teachers, elderly women we'd never seen before, were the tribunal. Before them we had to exhibit our wares, demonstrating precisely how we would introduce a child to the gold beads or the shoe-polishing basket, answering questions on the Montessori theory of child development, and having our notebooks criticized. Finally I was told I'd passed.

The eight-week program was only the beginning. A year of internship must follow, in which I would teach under a certified Montessori teacher. Then I would be eligible for my Montessori certificate — if and when I finished my bachelor's degree. (I finished it in August of 1969. The Montessori certificate arrived one day in September when I was doing something very un-Montessori-ish — running barefoot in the grass with the children in a fine hop-skip-and-jump led by Shirley. I looked at this large piece of paper and thought of a song Peggy Lee was just making famous: "Is that all there is?")

My year of internship began under a teacher who had had both European and American Montessori training. She made every day a continuing examination, reminiscent of the one I'd had at the end of the eight-week course. She was quite certain that no eight-week course could in any way prepare me to "be with children," as she put it. So I was an aide in the more demeaning sense of the word — a kind of policeman to move about the room saying "Choose some work, now" or "Sit down." I got the children in from the cars and got them out again a few hours later. Little else. After a month I was fed up with it, and said so. Very well, I was told. Mrs. X would teach me herself.

So began a series of painful afternoons. The one that sticks most in my mind may serve as an example of many of them. I was demonstrating how a good Montessori teacher waters the plants. You pick up the pitcher with the right hand, support the spout with your left hand, and raise the right and lower the left to pour. Then you remove the left hand from the spout and use it to grab the sponge, with which you wipe the last drop from the spout. The pitcher is placed on its tray just so, the sponge squeezed out in the little cup in the corner of the tray and placed in the lower left-hand corner of the tray. You then carry the tray with two hands, at waist level, to the shelf, move your hands forward, and put it down. Absolute clarity of movement, absolute precision in lifting, using, and placing objects — so that children will learn the one perfect way to water a philodendron. That afternoon I couldn't get the sponging right. Three tries. Then, "Mrs. Skutch, how can you consider yourself ready to Be with Children when you have not been trained to Wipe the Drop from the Spout with the Sponge?"

The implication was not only that I was incompetent. I'd been criminally mistrained. Fairleigh Dickinson had just declared its allegiance to the American Montessori Society rather than the Internazionale, and that pointed clearly to the root of my troubles: I'd been the victim of scheming upstarts. My mentor was certain of it when I failed another of her tests. I'd been scrubbing tables after school — not to show that I knew the sixteen steps, but because the tables were dirty. An intern was expected to polish up the handle on the big front door, as W. S. Gilbert put it. Out of that particular silence that lies heavily over a certain kind of schoolroom when the children have gone, my supervisor's voice thundered: "In what year did Maria Montessori establish the San Lorenzo experiment?"

I tried to think, then ventured a date in the first decade of the twentieth century. I was a year off. "Had you been correctly trained, you would have known that as you know your own name," I was told. I wondered for a minute what my own name was.

Very shortly thereafter, in one of Connecticut's colder Januaries, David and I were banging on the door of the Whitby

School in Greenwich. Thanks to many newspaper and magazine articles, Whitby is probably the best-known Montessori school in America. Nancy Rambusch had started it, but soon left to carry her Montessori crusade to heathen parts. After a little negotiation I arranged to continue my internship there and to have David entered as a pupil.

The atmosphere at Whitby was very different from that in the school where we'd spent the fall. The equipment was very much the same — the Montessori materials — but it was being used far more freely, particularly in the room in which I was working. My new supervisor was a woman of varied experience, more Bank Street College of Education in her outlook than traditional Montessori — a refreshing change. I found myself enthusiastic and happy. And it was during my first month at Whitby that it became clear to me I should start my own school.

Stamford could use a school like this one, I believed. To have to drive an hour or more to a Montessori school was just too much for many Stamford parents. Yet there was a real demand for good early childhood education, a demand that wasn't being met, or so my survey of a year before suggested. I could do something about that. A school like this one? I thought, made notes, drew plans. As the months went by, the school I visualized came to be something of a combination of the two schools in which I'd been interning. The Montessori materials would be used fully and well, with imagination and freedom, as I found them being used at Whitby. But there would be something of the order and discipline, the workmanlike attitude and the spirit it could generate, which I'd sensed in some of the groups at the other school and which I missed a little at Whitby.

Looking back from the vantage point of today, I wonder about these judgments. Would I still sense at Whitby that underlying rumble of not-quite-chaos; and if I did sense it, would I find it negative? Would I still see David's first school as workmanlike, or would I simply call it rigid? I'm not at ease with questions like these — lurking behind them is another question, "What will you think of what *you're* doing now, when *it's* five years in your past?" How sure we are we're right! How surely we prove later on to have been at best only half right!

But I felt very right that February. February 1965, late in the month. The newspaper clipping I saved doesn't carry the exact date — odd I shouldn't remember such a red-letter day. It's a two-column story, five inches in each column. Across the top, the *Stamford Advocate* proclaimed:

MONTESSORI SCHOOL PLANS
ANNOUNCED FOR STAMFORD

Eight

My First School

The newspaper story simply announced that the Montessori
School of Stamford was being formed. Those parents of pre-
school-age children who might be interested were asked to
telephone me. About a hundred did. I asked them to come to
either of two meetings to be held at one of the Stamford
churches — regrettably not the one at which I'd arranged to
rent basement space for the school, but enough of an approxima-
tion so that I'd be able to suggest what kind of an environment
for learning we could prepare. Looking over the list of names I

took down at those meetings, I find that almost everyone who came has had children at the school. Obviously I wasn't the only parent looking for a different kind of preschool education. I'd hit on a real community need.

I approached these meetings with fear and trembling. How presumptuous I was! A junior-college graduate, a former department-store buyer, an exurbanite housewife — why would any intelligent family wish to entrust to me the schooling of their children? I expected to be ridiculed, if not by the mothers and fathers who came to these meetings, then by my own better self. So when the first meeting went well, I was hardly reassured: the second must surely be a disaster. But not at all, it went swimmingly. Many parents took application forms away with them, and when they began sending them back I knew I was launched. Would I and the school prove seaworthy?

The meetings were times to talk about the school, to demonstrate some of the materials, to give parents a good look at me. I spoke of what I hoped the school would become, since it existed only as plans. I talked about Maria Montessori's ideas about education and how I thought we could apply them in the mid-1960's. As I talked, the room seemed to come alive with children I hadn't yet seen, at work in ways I could only imagine.

I was talking about something quite different from what I'd lived with during that first half year of internship. The incident of the watering pitcher and the sponge still rankled. The important thing, I said to myself, wasn't that one Wipe the Drop from the Spout with the Sponge; it was that one respect children and their learning, and help them respect and care for growing things as we cared for them. The great Maria Montessori would have agreed with me, I thought. (I was probably wrong about this. I think there are significant points at which I would disagree with her, were she and I able to meet and talk — disagree with genuine humility but also with some stubbornness. But when I was starting the school I wasn't clear about these disagreements. And, like many a novice, I very much needed to identify myself with a mother superior, even at the risk of distorting her beliefs and my own.)

The meetings had been preceded, and were followed, by a lot of activity. I was discovering things I'd never known anything about, for all my involvement with city politics. Let me tell you some things I learned which you ought to know if you're thinking of starting a school yourself.

Get in touch with your state department of education and find out what the rules are about chartering a school. Perhaps they can tell you everything you have to know. More likely, they will refer you for some matters to a city or town or county board of education. You'll find that there are dozens of things you have to pay attention to.

First, your site. Zoning comes in here, if your community is zoned. If you start in a church or synagogue — places often available for weekday use, with reasonable working space — you probably won't have any trouble from the zoning office. On the other hand, if you're using your own house, you may find yourself involved in a lot of argument, particularly if your school is "proprietary" — that is, owned and run by you as a business. Zoning boards are likely to look with greater favor on schools incorporated not for profit.

You'll probably find that a school building has to be surrounded by a certain amount of open play space. You may find regulations about the permissible slope of the land in relation to water supply and sewage disposal. If you're operating in temporary quarters it's possible you won't be required to meet some of the site standards, but you had better make sure.

Then there's the building itself. State and city officials are rightly concerned about fire safety, and their concern is expressed in very specific terms about fire escapes, fire drills, fire extinguishers, fire doors, and so on. Again, these may be less stringently enforced if you're in a temporary school building and can prove it's temporary. But for the sake of the children, satisfy yourself that you're not putting them in any danger.

There may be minimum standards for such things as the ratio of children to toilets, cubic feet of classroom space, or square feet of windows. Levels of lighting may be specified.

The calendar will probably be determined by minimum standards too: school should be open so many days a year — more if you like, but no fewer. Certain holidays may be mandatory. The minimum length of a school day could be a matter of regulation.

Some of the regulations apply to all schools, some only to schools for children of certain ages. In our preschool program, for two-to-five-year-olds, we are permitted to make our own calendar and set the length of the school day. On the other hand, we are bound by building and site specifications: masonry construction, thirty-five square feet of floor space per child inside, seventy-five square feet of playground space outside, a toilet for every fifteen children.

It was with such details that I found myself concerned as I went about planning the first year of a school which might never open, it seemed to me. I had had to give up the notion of having the school in a lovely old carriage house and go instead to a thirty-by-fifty-foot room in the basement of a church. And my view of a school where children might carry on projects over days or weeks got a jolt when I found we would have to pack the school away every afternoon so the building could serve those myriad other functions that make up a church program — scout meetings, Alcoholics Anonymous, an adult Bible class like the one I used to teach. At the meetings with prospective parents I was able to show them how we were planning to cope with this problem — and, incidentally, where much of my capital had gone.

Instead of our present low shelves, we had cabinets on casters, which could be rolled in and out of a storage closet. In our new building the shallow bays make natural divisions of space, but in the church basement we had to use folding screens. It took us an hour each morning to turn the room into a school — Isobel, then as now our aide, Charlie, the high-school boy who helped us then as Bruce does now, and me. That's how I got into the habit of getting to school an hour early. What's now bridge-building time was hard labor that first year.

After the meetings I began interviewing the parents who'd filled out application forms. Why the parents rather than the children? I guess it had to do with my sense that I knew relatively little about children. I enjoyed teaching them, I felt myself very much on their side in the ongoing battle for understanding, knowledge, and skill, but when it came to making sound judgments about who should and who should not be in my school, I felt very incompetent. I thought, perhaps naïvely, that the parents could help me know their children and thus give me a basis on which to make decisions.

I know better than that now. As I've suggested earlier, schools like ELC can be good places for children from many, many backgrounds, with all sorts of endowments, and with a considerable spectrum of problems, from Janie's perfectionism to Ann Louise's tantrums. It would be arbitrary to try to select among them: there isn't a child who doesn't need good education.

But one can do some selecting — if selecting is necessary — among parents. I interview them today not for the information they can give me about Peter or Mary, but so I can get some sense of the homes Peter and Mary live in and from which they would come to school each day. I have to try to do something far more difficult than assessing a child's readiness for the best educational system we can make for him: I must try to weigh what he would most certainly gain from that education against what he would be experiencing at home, as it might undercut, contradict, or insidiously destroy his gains.

I selected our twenty-two families in these home visits. And on a bright, autumn-crisp day in late September, twenty-five children trooped into the church basement, my first pupils.

I look back at the school from today's vantage point, and it's hard to recognize it as the first stage of the Early Learning Center. I've spoken of my concern about the outdoors and my attempt to control the amount of time the children would spend outside. I had a great fear that unless I was hovering over every child every minute he might not be learning. Convinced that children are able to learn many concepts and skills much earlier than they do in the public schools, I was very much aware of my role as teacher and of the school as *school*.

Take the matter of the desks. I'd heard that New York City had a lot of surplus elementary-school desks available for next to nothing. Indeed, they did. Most of them were in secondhand furniture stores, though, spread throughout the five boroughs of the city. We got several station-wagon loads of them, sawed off legs where it was necessary, and sprayed them with enamel — yellow for the underbody, white for the top, to match the yellow-and-white polyurethane chairs I'd brought home a few weeks earlier. I was proud of those desks and chairs, and how their colors brightened the basement room with its puce-pink walls and mud-brown floor. I was proud of the compliments I received from two Connecticut elementary-school principals who visited one day. Now I think I was being complimented for just the wrong thing: I'd successfully imposed an order on the children rather than helping them discover conceptual order. I had children of three and four doing what they usually don't do until six in Connecticut — sitting at desks studying. The desks are in the big barn now. Maybe we'll find a use for them one day. A few of the chairs are in the school, but not many.

We made some false generalizations on the basis of that first year. One was that the children of staff members should never be allowed to enroll. We'd all had children in the school that year, and we'd found it hard for us and hard for them. I even wrote a rule about it: *No teacher's child in the classroom.* As with the desks, I wasn't seeing the real issue. We were terribly — I choose the adverb with some care — concerned with having an orderly place for the children to learn and hadn't yet discovered the real sources of order. Our own children recognized our subtle, concealed (sometimes from ourselves) attempts to impose order and told us in their various ways that they weren't buying it.

I've learned since then of many situations in which the children of staff members have profited enormously from attending the schools their parents teach in. These situations have one factor in common: the staff members know what they're doing and why they're doing it. When things go wrong — as they did our first year — it's because the teachers are unsure of themselves; because their ideas about education exist more as words than as actions; because they're trying to live something that isn't really natural to them. Children sense artificiality very quickly. A child who doesn't know you very well may just decide to make the best of it. Your own child won't be so patient.

Another of our generalizations was that there were precise formulas for dealing with children. I wrote down phrases to be used — ten "Principles for Tone and Its Expression in Language." (How ubiquitous is the influence of the decimal system on our thinking!) A few samples:

3. Give the social reason for rules rather than flat authority:
   "Put it back for the next person."
   rather than
   "Put your work away."

5. Be specific. Give concrete information using concrete names and commands:
   "If you hold the card by its edge, it will stay clean."
   rather than
   "Don't mess up the cards."

9. Recognize the validity of emotions when you limit destructive actions:
   "I know you are *angry*, but you may not hurt Mary."

rather than

"Why did you hit Mary? She is your friend."

I'm afraid this kind of thing came from my Montessori training, where the emphasis was — as the *Encyclopaedia Britannica*
puts it — on "the precise and best way" of doing whatever it
was one was doing with children, so that they wouldn't form
"an imperfect habit." Thank goodness for learning — my learning! What I came to understand was that it was the attitude, the
fundamental belief about what children are like and how they
learn, which is of vital importance. I expect I still say a lot of
things like those I wrote down. I've spoken of my general rule
about avoiding praise and blame, and about attaching our few
school regulations to specific instances. But I hope these come
out of a real sense of what children are about, not out of some
notion of what a teacher ought to be.

Let me digress for a minute to suggest that there's a real
difference between training and education. Training is useful if
the desired outcome is a specific set of skills or behaviors, but
the emphasis all too often remains on the skills and behaviors
rather than on what must underlie them. Education is concerned
with the underlying things — with who and what you are, where
you're going, what you do with what you know. Well-trained,
I had a set of verbal responses ready to draw upon and to set
down for others. I wasn't yet educated enough to realize that
words are useful only when they are deeply felt and when the
deep feelings arise from the situation in which the words are
spoken. And then they may not be necessary at all.

From that first year, I remember trying to use my training with
Freddie. For the third or fourth day he'd gone to the table where
we had art materials and started to spread paints around. I'd
spoken to him about the paper and the brush and the water
pot ("Hold the brush like this, moisten it in the water, like
this . . .") and demonstrated the movements as clearly as I could,

but it hadn't made much impression. Now I was trying to interest him in something else, the cylinders. Again I was being as precise as I could — the clear hand movements, the direct and simple explanation. No response. Talking about this with Larry Schneider, our psychologist, I suddenly realized that I was worried mainly because my training wasn't paying off, not because of what Freddie was or wasn't doing. The problem was with my pride, my status. So I took another look at Freddie. The paints interested him but he wasn't ready for them. What might he be ready for? I got out some scraps of colored paper and some mucilage, laid out a big sheet of newsprint, and invited Freddie to cut and paste.

So began the collage table. Before long it had a round top, divided pie-fashion into four segments, each painted a different color. In each segment there was a box for scraps, a pair of scissors, a glue brush, and a jar of mucilage, color-coded in Montessori fashion so they'd be easy to keep in that segment. Into the boxes went bits of paper, cloth, string, even chips of wood. Often there were four children working around the table. Freddie was usually one of them. For most of this first year — ours and his — collage was his major activity. Then he was ready to move on to other things. It was part of my education to learn that however much I wanted to be the ideal Montessori teacher, a child like Freddie simply didn't want to be — or at least wasn't — the ideal Montessori child.

Larry Schneider has been our consulting psychologist from the beginning, and it's to his presence at staff meetings and parent conferences that I owe a great deal of my education. Today we use him to lead sensitivity training groups for the faculty, an hour a week. (Recently a group of parents has started a similar series of group meetings with Larry as chairman.) He helps us become more sensitive to each other, to the children and their parents, to ourselves as we examine our own behaviors. Sometimes the meetings have a lot to do with what's been going on in the school that week, or with a particular incident we've been troubled by. Sometimes they have nothing at all to do with the school — except that we are the teachers in the school, who bring to it each day our feelings and thoughts. We turn to Larry when we have specific problems with specific children. Often enough, as with Freddie, we find the problem isn't in the child but in ourselves. Larry's work with parents helps them, and through them their children. Such a person is a great asset to a school, worth much in time and money.

I had the service of another consultant the first two years of the school, a very important kind of person for someone who is newly a school director. Rosa Packard was a wonderfully skillful Montessori teacher, the best kind of critic a novice could have. She came to the school two days a week and sat and watched, and then gave me her opinion of what I was doing right and what I was doing wrong. Then she came to meetings of the faculty — Isobel, my friend Jane, who taught French, and I — and helped the three of us look seriously at what the school was doing. This was enormously helpful. As I would urge any school director to get a good psychological consultant, so I would urge the importance of having an educational consultant, at least for the first few years the school is in operation. Who? Someone the director believes in enough to have faith in, take guidance from. In our case, it was a Montessori expert. In yours, it might be someone from a completely different orientation — your orientation, or at least one very close to yours.

Rosa Packard was very much concerned with the teacher as a model. Much of what she had to say to me about this was in terms of my handling of Montessori materials: a reminder that the way in which I dealt with the pink tower, for instance, was the way the children would deal with it. If I wanted them to appreciate the single isolated concept (the relationships among cubes of graduated sizes) which the pink tower incorporates, then it was important that I handle the cubes precisely, and in such a way that the children could see exactly what I was doing.

This was, of course, what my first internship supervisor had been trying to teach me. But what a difference! Now, instead of being trained in a ritual, I was being helped to understand something about how children learn. Rosa wasn't saying that there is one perfect way to build the pink tower. She was saying that well-thought-out learning materials may need careful handling when they are first introduced to children, if the children are to get the most from them. But more than that, she was pointing out to me that when a child learns a new behavior, he does so by looking for an example of it to copy — a grown-up example, if he can find one. I apply this in wider areas. If I don't want the children dashing through the school, then I mustn't dash when the telephone rings. If I speak quietly and politely to the children, they're likely to speak quietly and politely — more likely, at any rate, than if I yell at them. For young children in particular, teachers are persons to emulate.

This is an isolated example of something gleaned from a consultant, and not a very important example, perhaps. I mention it simply to suggest that the help you get from a good consultant isn't limited to the specific matters on which you consult him. Many of my insights about children have come from discussions with Larry Schneider about quite other children. Talking with him about Janie's home and the pressures she brought to school from it helped me understand how Ann Louise's behavior reflects things going on at her home — very different things in a very different home.

There's a third kind of consultation that's often useful. I read about a meeting of educators at which the Leicestershire schools would be discussed. I knew very little about Leicestershire, only that the movement had produced some attractive learning materials which were turning up in equipment catalogues. But I was interested and thought I should find out more. So I went. Anyone looking at the Early Learning Center today — particularly by comparison with the Montessori School of Stamford in 1964 — will know how important that meeting was for me.

I consulted some of the people there, and I asked them to visit the school. They did, and as the years have gone by I've had many of the English schoolmen responsible for this new movement in elementary education come by for a day or two. And I've visited their schools, and the schools in this country with which some of them have been connected. Perhaps I should call this occasional consultation, to differentiate it from regular consultation. Occasional consultation is often a very useful shot in the arm — a new point of view, new insights, recognitions of things that need to be done or changed.

Perhaps it's unnecessary to say so, but it's one of those ideas which are given lip service far more often than they're lived: *schools must be places where teachers as well as children learn and grow.* An educational institution must be educational for everybody concerned with it, if it's really to do its job. My occasional consultants have taught me a great deal. Now that I'm an occasional consultant myself, I have a chance to see a lot of schools, and see them with a somewhat practiced eye. One of the things I notice is the great difference between a school in which the teachers are learning as well as the children (and often from them) and a school in which adult learning has died — if, indeed, it was ever alive.

We run a better school today than we did then. But I'm not ashamed of that first year. We were all learning, children and teachers — and parents, too, those wonderful parents who worked so hard when we needed them. Perhaps even the consultants learned from our struggles and our problems.

A good year. A hard year.

A harder one was to come.

Nine

To Be or Not to Be

Or, to go to another of Shakespeare's plays:

> *There is a tide in the affairs of men,*
> *Which, taken at the flood, leads on to fortune;*
> *Omitted, all the voyage of their life*
> *Is bound in shallows and in miseries.*
> *On such a full sea are we now afloat,*

And we must take the current when it serves,
Or lose our ventures.

I expect it's true of most new projects — you reach a point where you have to go all out or close. It was obvious we were approaching that point in the second year of the Montessori School of Stamford.

The church basement just wasn't good enough. Packing the school away every noon was an exhausting chore. Putting up wrapping-paper murals to cover the Boy Scout awards bulletin board, one of the features of the gray-pink room, wasn't such a challenge anymore — as a matter of fact, it was a deadly bore for both teachers and children. That wasn't all, by a long shot. We'd run short of money because we weren't skillful budget makers, and we'd had to invent an assortment of fund-raising activities — a book fair, a toy fair, a dance — no one of which had raised very much money. (One of the biggest-and-best toy companies gave us only ten percent off, so the $3,000 worth of their products we sold netted us only $300. A less-known company — later absorbed by the biggest-and-best — gave us forty percent.) Then we were under pressure to take more children. A number of parents had held off during the school's first year, to see whether we'd sink, I suppose. Who can blame them? With a good year behind the school, they wanted to enroll their children. We took some of them, but there wasn't room for them all.

Added to all of this was my own sense that I needed more education. I needed it for purely practical purposes — I wouldn't be a certified Montessori teacher until I had a bachelor's degree. But I needed it for its own sake, too. Visitors to the school during its first year had spoken familiarly of ideas about education of which I knew nothing or next to nothing. Some of them sounded like important ideas. I was coming to realize that Maria Montessori hadn't said it all.

So it was go or no go, fish or cut bait, as they put it on the

New England coast. "We must take the current when it serves, or lose our ventures."

A critical need was money. The problem had begun with the opening of the school; it had become complicated by our success. With the help of a friendly banker we'd managed to raise enough to buy the property the school now stands on (I'd bought the house and an acre of land; the school had bought the rest of the land). This had left us heavily in debt and without any notion of how to put up a building. I'd spent hours in the Foundation Library on Madison Avenue in New York, a suite of decorator-modern rooms full of information about organizations with money to give away. Unfortunately, there didn't seem to be any organization interested in supporting a tiny nursery school with big ideas. But I had come upon the listing of the Educational Facilities Laboratories.

EFL is one of the many offshoots of the Ford Foundation. EFL supports research in designing facilities for education, as their title suggests. I visited their secretary-treasurer, Jonathan King, then Harold Gores, the president. They made it very clear EFL couldn't put up a building for us. "We don't put money into anything you can kick," said Gores. But they were interested in supporting research. In Stamford we spent weeks putting together a research proposal. We would undertake to write the specifications for a fifty-pupil preschool building, in terms of the needs of children, the learning process, and what could be determined of the activities and equipment made necessary by them, and we would work with an architect in turning these specifications into plans. EFL granted us $4,000.

The quandary was the outcome of this research. We had a magnificent building — on paper. It would cost something like a quarter of a million dollars to build. None of the multi-million-dollar corporations in Stamford could see their way to making substantial contributions, and all the wealthy individuals I knew or knew of were already overcommitted. We wrote a final report on our research project, added a set of the plans, and posted it off with a thank-you note to the Educational Facilities Laboratories. And sat upon the ground to tell sad stories.

February is a terrible month in New England, particularly for a Virginian. It was time to send out enrollment forms for the coming year to the parents of our thirty children, but I delayed. I was becoming more and more certain there wouldn't be a coming year.

Into this dark scene suddenly there came a flood of light. Enter a heroine, Phyllis, my secretary. On a visit to Cambridge, Massachusetts — suitably enough, that hard winter, to go to a funeral — she idly scanned the listing of architects in the yellow pages of the phone book. There she came on Componoform, a modular design process, and the name of Egon Ali-Oglu. Remembering some talk about modular design and building — working with standard-size units, as a child does with building blocks — she dialed Egon's number, called on him, talked briefly of our need for a building we couldn't afford.

His response excited her enough for her to call me in Stamford. "I think we can do it!" she said. "I found an architect in the yellow pages!" And she went on to speak of a precast concrete building that would be extremely attractive, to judge by photographs of a number of Componoform structures, that could be erected in a matter of weeks, and that would be almost unbelievably low in cost. I called our board of trustees. April 8, 1967, we sat down in Cambridge with Egon. The hero was upon the scene.

We met Egon at a time in his life when he was very much caught up in the problem of good education. As a teacher of architecture, he was experimenting with learning materials much as we were; like us, he was finding that when students are given freedom to learn in a rich environment, they teach themselves a great deal. He was fascinated by the parallels between his work with graduate students and ours with pre-primary children. He read our EFL report with enthusiasm, grunted sometimes approvingly, sometimes disapprovingly, over the plans of the building we couldn't build, and began that kind of talking-with-the-pencil architects indulge in. Very quickly we engaged him. Within a month we had set ourselves up as contractors. Within two months building was under way.

We'd solved the building problem through the yellow pages. My educational problem I solved in a manner quite as coincidental. The *Stamford Advocate* carried a feature story that winter about a local foot doctor who had gone back to college in his middle fifties because he'd always wanted a liberal arts education. He'd found the liberal arts education to be truly revolutionary: it had introduced him to a whole new world of ideas, responsibilities, potentials. The revolution had been possible because the college program was one in which he planned his own studies and carried them out very much on his own, with the help — when he needed it — of college faculty members.

Freedom to learn. Reading the story, I was at first struck by the similarity of this kind of education to what I was trying to do with the children, the kind of parallel Egon was to comment on a few months later. And then it occurred to me that this was the way *I* learned best. I'd used consultants just as the Stamford podiatrist had used college faculty members. The program was run by "Goddard College, a tiny experimental institution in the village of Plainfield, Vermont," the story said. I wrote for information. Late in that dark winter I went to Plainfield for the first two-week residential session of my two and a half years in the Goddard College Adult Degree Program.

Revolutionary? Perhaps for me more evolutionary. But how the Early Learning Center today differs from the Montessori School of Stamford in its first two years is in very large part due to what happened to me as I carried on my Goddard studies.

So ended this dramatic second year. I had never worked harder in my life. In the spring I was teaching every morning, serving as general contractor, fund raiser, and counselor to parents in the afternoons, and studying in the evenings. It was too much. I had to extend my first semester of Goddard studies to a full year. But the building was going up — in spite of a bomb threat from a disgruntled subcontractor and a physical attack on Egon in an argument with a supplier over the quality of some materials. I'd sent out the enrollment forms, announced that we would have a new home with room for twenty more children, and was busy much of the summer interviewing the parents of many more children than that.

I look back at that year — the image of Egon sitting on the floor of the church basement to see the world as a preschooler sees it; myself on a day of chilly rain holding on to my plastic raincoat with one hand while I tried to wield a spade with the other at our groundbreaking; a night I never got to bed, so fascinated had I become with reading A. S. Neill's *Summerhill*. There was my introduction to Synectics and to Peter Bergson — later to be our teacher of six-to-nine-year-olds, who was then a member of the Synectics team — as we were helped to use that problem-solving method with its brainstorming and its argument by analogy and metaphor in coping with our financial headaches. There was the day I sat down to write a letter to the parents saying the school wouldn't — couldn't — go on next year. And couldn't write the letter.

Suddenly a flood of other images. The children so very happy in the tiny backyard of that church basement. Marilyn, a child I've lost track of, curled up in the pretty reading corner we'd made out of folding screens, bright printed fabric, an old rocking chair. Freddie teaching Rosemary how to use the mucilage bottle at the collage table. A dark afternoon in January when we were all feeling very sorry for ourselves as we put the school away for the day — and then, for no reason, started giggling, the three of us, and couldn't stop. My first journey to Cambridge, dangerously close to April Fool's Day (was I on a fool's errand?), and my discovery of the special world of Harvard Square. Another first journey — to the surplus stores of Canal Street in Manhattan, with gratitude to Nancy Rambusch for having suggested that it was proper and useful to invent one's own learning equipment.

It was my first school, as important and irreplaceable as any first. I left it gladly for the new building, but the images remain.

Ten

We Make a Name
for Ourselves

A small circus visited Stamford last summer. Walking towards
its big top with David and Christopher I was struck by how
much our school building looks like a great tent, a tent with
no central pole. Coming into the school, you see that the
peaked roof is a skylight, over a great open expanse of carpeted
floor. But the poles — the precast concrete columns which are
the bones of the Componoform system — aren't hard to find.

Our educational aim is to make concepts clear to children.

Egon's design makes the structure of the building abundantly clear. The columns are eminently visible, each with its four short horizontal crossbeams radiating at right angles from its top. The joints between the crossbeams and the tie beams which join them are clear, too. Architects speak of "curtain walls" in this kind of construction, and the tent analogy again seems apt. My children and I watched the lightweight wall sections being put into place. Egon showed us the insides of one — a two-inch-thick sandwich with polystyrene foam (one of the best insulators) in the middle and cement-asbestos board on the outsides.

When I first talked with Egon I asked him if we could have lots of windows.

"You can have windows everywhere, if you want," he said.

Would we be able to add to the building if the school grew?

"Not more than sixteen more stories!" he said. And then he demonstrated with miniature components how the walls might be solid or all glass; the doors, or windows, of any size or shape; and how column could be joined to column, up and up, and floor slab joined to floor slab for expansion outwards. "You want another room? We take out the wall panels, make a slab, put up two more columns, slip on a roof!" He was moving parts around on the floor of his studio. "You want to put the new room on top? We take the roof off, stick in a floor slab, add four columns, tiebeams, panels, stick the roof back on — see?"

That's what our plans call for now, as we move to build for the primary group. It will be a natural growth, because the potential for it is cast into the Componoform system.

The skylight is over what we call the core area. An early newspaper note about the building describes it as "a constant reference point for the children and teachers, both indoors and out" and adds that it "contains the equipment," which simply demonstrates how hard it is to put a place into words. Let me try again: The core area is a big open floor covered with carpet, about twenty-four feet square. It's marked off not by walls but by the low shelves on which we keep the learning materials. In Egon's original plan six of my secondhand school desks are sketched in, arranged somewhat at random. They aren't there in actuality: Danny dumps the Unifix cubes on the floor, where he builds his trains, and it is on the floor that Alice and her friends sit to play concentration.

On three sides of the core — north, east, and west, approximately — there are spaces of about equal size, so the building has a T-shaped floor plan. The western bay is the grown-up space, shut off from the core by the one-way vision screen, where the visitors hide. The other two bays we originally called classrooms, and in his sketch plan Egon has them filled with desks and chairs, arranged in groups of two or three. Once again, they're not there, and the spaces bear little resemblance to classrooms in any usual sense of the word. The eastern bay is the "sensorium," a place for sensory experiences of all the various kinds Shirley has concerned herself with. She has a great assortment of musical instruments — bells, marimbas, drums, zithers, and so on. There is a phonograph, on a wheeled cart so it can be moved around the school. On a big table are the modeling materials. Another big table is for painting. There's a hot plate for cooking simple things for the tasting exercises — or just for the fun of cooking. At each side a door leads to the outdoors. The northern bay we've used for many things. During the fall and winter of 1969–1970 it had a dress-up corner featuring a big oval mirror surrounded by light bulbs. The Bonnie Prudden gym set has been there, too, and the Wendy House.

But this is a building we can change as we need to. By spring of this year it had become clear we needed a special place for the almost-sixes. What kind of a place? First, a place somewhat separate from the rest of the school, because one of these children's major needs is to feel that there's distinction in being older. Second, a place which would be planned to serve some of their distinguishing characteristics: their greater physical strength and agility, their ability to read or at least to use books independently and intelligently, and their relative sophistication in projects using abstractions (numbers and words) on the one hand, tools and materials on the other.

So the northern bay was walled off with plywood, except for a narrow opening. The main approach is via a ladder — actually a number of foot-size holes, one above the other — to a height of about five feet, where there's a larger hole through which a child can wriggle (or an adult can squeeze) onto a shag-carpeted, rope-railed catwalk. From the catwalk one may descend by other ladders into one of three rooms. The first, walled with mirrored Mylar to make it look twice its small size, we've used for a variety of building projects. Its main furniture is a workbench, its main equipment is wood, wire, various tools. The second room also has a workbench, but it's for adding machines, a calculator, and a full-size electric typewriter — gifts from a local office-machines company. The third room I call the book garden. Books are on shelves, on racks hanging from the walls, on the windowsills. There are chairs and cushions and a soft rug to curl up on while you read.

Bright colors, interesting shapes, the challenge of the catwalk and the ladders: very much a special place. The younger children have looked in, but they respect what we've simply stated, not as a rule but as a fact, that this is the older children's space. Total cost? A couple of hundred dollars, time spent in scavenging materials, a weekend of carpentry, a number of evenings painting and finishing. In another weekend we could change the space back into an open bay, and save most of the materials for a later project.

A general principle emerges. Don't tie yourself to a rigid floor plan with immovable walls. Better the movable screens and wheeled cabinets of our first church basement. Better yet, the great flexibility of Egon's Componoform building. A prepared environment is at its best a dynamic one, changing to meet the changing needs of children.

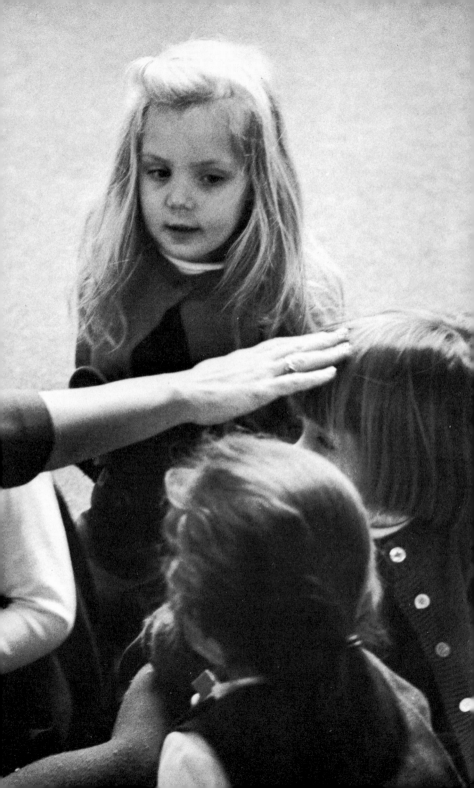

A detail or two about the school building as a whole. The main heat is electric, from baseboard convectors. There is electric radiant heat from the floor if we need it, but we've never turned it on, as the baseboard heating does such a good job. Over every door there's a small fan-forced electric heater, thermostatically controlled, to take care of that blast of cold air when a child goes in or out on a winter day. The carpeting is the indoor-outdoor kind you can wash if something is spilled. It's one of those neutral colors, a gray which doesn't show soil easily.

We could have had cabinets built for storage and display of the materials. Instead, because we wanted the room to be easy to rearrange, we used cinder blocks with long, wide boards. The boards and blocks are heavy enough so that a child can't knock a shelf over. Both the blocks and the boards take paint easily; but they look well unpainted too. Most of the lighting is from museum lights — small reflector units mounted on a track ten feet or so above the floor. The units themselves can be moved along the track, to cluster lights where they're needed, and each unit swivels. The light is from incandescent bulbs, and is far softer than fluorescent light would be. Some neurologists claim it's more healthy, too — they say the flickering of fluorescent tubes can trigger migraines or convulsions.

We originally intended the Forum area — that conversation pit in front of the one-way vision screen — as a place for group instruction. But we've moved away from group instruction since then, and the Forum has become a favorite reading place, where children read to themselves or to one or two others. There are other reading places, too: a rocking chair by a window, for instance, and a low table at which a child can sit in one of the remaining white-and-yellow chairs and the book garden.

Everything that needs to be child-size is. Toilets and washbasins are low. So are clothes pegs, doorknobs, bookshelves. In every way we can make it so, the building is part of the prepared environment for learning. It doesn't simply house the learning materials and activities; it is part of them and they are part of it.

We sent plans of the building to the Educational Facilities Laboratories. They sent people to talk to Egon and me about the planning and construction. They saw that two quite different designs could be developed from the same set of specifications — and one of them at a third the cost of the other. Jonathan King of EFL was interested in the Componoform system of building good schools. He was also interested in the flowering of what had at one point seemed so withered a project — our step-by-step move from the nature of child life and learning to the hard facts of concrete and steel. "We ought to show people how this gets done," he said.

And almost before we knew it, he had a camera crew and a director spending day after day with us. The result was a twenty-minute sound film in color showing the school in operation, focusing on some of its architectural details, and illustrating the manufacture and assembly of the precast concrete components. Later EFL granted additional funds to circulate the film, called *Room to Learn*.

We were becoming known. Architects and educators came to call. The building was something of a landmark, and since the building was intimately related to what went on inside it, the program was getting a lot of attention too. In the most direct and literal sense we made ourselves a name. The school had become a center for the work of many specialists concerned with the way children learn in the early years — a clinical psychologist; an architect and his associates and students; consultants on learning materials, pedagogy, and child development; concerned and committed parents; and our small, hard-working faculty. A center for work in early learning. We decided to call it the Early Learning Center. It was a more accurate name for this three-year-old institution. The Montessori School of Stamford was gone forever.

The new building made possible a project I'd had in mind since my summer of training at Fairleigh Dickinson. There should be better ways of educating teachers. Rather than lectures and tests, the ritual handling of learning materials, and the occasional silent observation of children who mustn't look at us, I had the notion of a program which would have its heart in a working schoolroom.

We would not attempt to train teachers. Rather, we'd help them look at children, work with children, sit beside children; then they would talk with each other and with us about what they saw and thought. We'd bring in some experts for discussions — regular consultants and occasional consultants. We'd try to get people with different points of view and let the student teachers come to their own conclusions. So began our ELC workshops. There are two sessions each summer, each three weeks long, and recently we held a midwinter session. For the summer workshops we limit the groups to eight or ten persons each. Their main resource is a school of twenty-five children taught by our own staff. The workshop faculty includes me, another full-time teacher with a point of view at least slightly different from mine, one or two regular consultants, and a lot of occasional consultants.

The first summer I had Ruth Obolensky and Nancy Rambusch, two of my Fairleigh Dickinson instructors, working with me. The emphasis was on Montessori and what one might develop from the Montessori system, but we invited other points of view, and a number of them were represented among our occasional consultants.

For the second summer we had two emphases. One was Synectics, a method through which a group (children, faculty members, a family) can work together on whatever problems come up in the group; Peter Bergson was my consultant on this. The other emphasis was the Leicestershire system, and we had a great many consultants who were or had been connected with those British schools.

In the 1970 workshops we were concerned with American schools, from as practical a point of view as possible. We were looking at what was going on and what could go on in the public schools, and at the large number of federally funded projects. We were talking about foundations and how to prepare grant requests or research proposals. Among the occasional consultants were John Holt and Hiam Ginnot, to talk with us about how each of them works with children — contemporary American children.

Perhaps it's artificial to speak of Synectics and the Leicestershire system as emphases. They are, more accurately, connecting themes for our talks with consultants. The basic emphasis is always on the children and the student teachers and how they can relate to each other to foster learning and understanding in both groups.

I suppose we began making a name for ourselves when we threw all of the time and energy we had into making a school out of a church basement, and were young enough, strong enough, idealistic enough to do it every day, day after day, for two years and part of a third. To people who had never thought about it before, we were saying you don't just make a school and then teach in it, you remake it constantly. An environment for learning isn't prepared once and for all; it's always in a state of becoming.

We went on making our name — and lost the support of some persons in the process, I'm sorry to say — when we began helping children to use the Montessori materials in their own ways rather than in the ways prescribed by orthodox Montessori teachers and trainers. We added materials and activities of our own. We added an element of freedom and faced the difficult questions which appear when you try to define freedom and relate it to discipline, control, responsibility, and maturing.

Then came the building, the film, the stream of visitors, and the workshops. The Early Learning Center has indeed become something of a center for people interested in early learning — not only for ourselves and those we work with most directly, but for a far wider audience.

It's this fact and my own insatiable curiosity that has sent me back to school again. This time it's the Antioch-Putney Graduate School. (I didn't realize until very recently that Will Hamlin, my coauthor, got his M.A. from the same institution, before it became part of Antioch College.) Antioch-Putney students have visited the Early Learning Center frequently, and we may make some formal internship arrangements with them.

After the M.A.? I don't know. I can't imagine that I won't be involved with some kind of adult education. A doctorate? Not just for the sake of the degree, certainly. But there's so much I don't know about child growth and development, particularly the development of language. Our regular consultations with Larry about the children in the school have interested me in the part that deep emotions play in learning — Janie's need to please, Ann Louise's fear of loss, Jerry's panic at feeling squashed and squeezed by women. A. S. Neill's ideas about freedom fascinate me, and I'd like to investigate a way of setting them in the context of my own developing theory of learning and what I sense of the dependence of all persons on each other and on all the processes and materials of the world. Much of this I could learn on my own — am learning, to the extent that defining a problem involves learning. But I need help, too, and the right kind of graduate program might be a way of getting some of that help.

I would like the Early Learning Center to have a very good name for itself. This means it has to be the best school I can make it. I aim to keep trying.

Eleven

Today

I get up early on school mornings. In the spring the sun's up before me, but often there's still dew on the grass when I leave the house. I want to be at school at least an hour before the children arrive, at nine. There's a morning coolness in the air as I walk that country path, but the sun promises a warm day. It lights the oyster white of the school's walls to an almost yellow brightness, and it splashes on some of the children's paintings

I've taped to a floor-to-ceiling window. In the north bay it lights up the colors of the older children's book garden.

My bridge building this morning has to do with those fives and sixes, Ann Louise's group. How she's flowered in this garden! I'm again reminded of how important it can be for these children to have something of their own, something to affirm their greater maturity. And then I think about their other great need, for reassurance that they're "really learning." I remember an adult student at Goddard who was preparing himself to teach science. His work was self-directed, largely self-evaluated, carried on independently with occasional teacher conferences. He said from time to time that he didn't think he was "really learning," he was just going through the motions in order to get the degree he needed. Then he took some science tests and found that by national standards he was way ahead of the bunch — and suddenly he realized that he had indeed been learning. He just needed to have it pointed out.

So it is with some of these children. Five-year-old Allan has just finished reading *The Paper Airplane Book,* the report of *Scientific American*'s half-serious, half-just-for-fun paper airplane contest. He read it because he wanted to make some of the paper airplanes — read it well and with understanding. But he doesn't *know* he can read. Allan runs into first graders who live near his house. "I'm in the purple reader," one of them says. "Boy, is it hard!" To help Allan in a situation like that, we have to let him know that he's reading too, and reading material way beyond the purple reader. So we must find occasions to point this out to him. "You've read all the airplane book, Allan. I like that!" Or, "What a big book, Allan. And you've read it all."

We're trying to do the same kind of thing with math. Our children have moved from Unifix cubes to the golden beads to some Catherine Stern materials to Cuisenaire rods and, finally, to turning their conceptual knowledge of quantity and proportion and relationship into numbers and other symbols. (Actually, they're well on their way to algebra.) We have to help them realize that what they've been doing is just what their public-school friends are talking about — adding, subtracting, finding sets, grouping and regrouping, and all the lingo of the new math — and that they've been doing more of it, at a more complex level. So we put things into words now, things we've not talked about before, to confirm to the five-and-a-half-year-old that he's really studying, really "learning."

This is the bridge we've built, with hammers and nails and lumber and paint, in the north bay; and with our words and ideas, as we talk with Allan and Ann Louise and the other eight children of this group.

The schoolroom is bright with sun, quiet, full of latent activity. I look around at the materials to see what needs ordering or arranging. Adam has been interested in the cutout letters. I must make sure to spend some time with him. He's put a G into the C compartment, and the M's and W's are all confused. I straighten them out. We'll try the sandpaper letters. Janie has filed a precise and delicate painting of a beetle in the box where we ask children to put papers they'd like us to look at. I must talk with her about how a beetle moves — hers, predictably enough, seems as frozen as an Egyptian scarab.

The six-to-nine group will be meeting at my house. Can I raise the money for the beautiful addition Egon has designed? I wonder again: should we simply concentrate on the two-to-five-year-olds, whom we know so much about, and develop further our special program for the transitionals, the five-and-a-halfs? Some days I'm very much moved that way. Then I visit an elementary school, or a family with elementary-school children, and I'm absolutely certain that we must continue the older group, and grow with the children until they're at least twelve — so much that could happen and should happen for these children isn't happening at all.

My desk. Will there be a half hour today to answer correspondence? Whatever happened to the notion that I'd spend two solid hours every afternoon doing office work, and that that would take care of the school-director part of my role? Yesterday: a useful meeting with Ann Louise's mother, but a sad one too. She and her husband are separating, probably divorcing. Well, I know that one, all right. I wish she'd spoken about it earlier; it might have helped us work with Ann Louise. Then there was a telephone call from Massachusetts: a nursery-school teacher would like to visit the school, and were there other places she should visit at the same time? I mentioned Whitby. An almost hysterical woman called to ask if she could enter her child in the school immediately, and she didn't want to take no for an answer (nor did I really want to give it, remembering my need to get David into Whitby such a few years, such a long way, back), and I made an appointment for some time — when? — this afternoon . . . perhaps I wrote it down. The two hours and more were gone. The mail wasn't answered.

Shall I look for a director and go back to being a full-time teacher? Go back? I've never been there. I went directly from apprenticeship into this complicated, exhausting, wonderful life. But shouldn't I simplify it now? I love the morning with the children. But I love being in charge, too — conferences with Egon, consultations with Larry, being responsible for thinking out and working out such projects as this new inner space. I even like doing the correspondence — when I can find time for it.

Carrie and Shirley have come in. I hope it's meant as much to these two women to be here as it has to the school. We don't agree on everything, but I doubt that any three hard-working, involved teachers ever would. Each of us brings a whole and unique personality into the school, and unique persons are by definition different from each other. I expect the children profit from the diversity; I'm sure they profit from the very total involvement of caring persons in preparing a good environment for learning.

Danny arrives, the first of the children. For a moment I'm surprised he's not wearing a jacket, and then it flashes on me that the year's almost over, summer's nearly here. Some of the children will be leaving for other schools, one or two for other parts of the world. Next year we will have very few children left who knew the school in its church-basement days, and none in another year. I'm happy about what we've done for most of the children. Happy for all of them in the sense that we gave them a warm, interesting, beautiful place to spend part of their lives in. But we worked better with some than with others, and I have a few regrets.

Could we have done more for Janie? What will happen to her in a school which daily reinforces her rigidity, provides no time for her quiet research into natural things, and limits and regulates the ways in which she can work out her tensions?

Ann Louise will go on with us, I learned yesterday. I have high hopes for her. Marna's beautiful intervention, an act of great sensitivity and compassion, broke her cycle of tantrums. Carrie's request for help with the little ones gave Ann Louise a role. The special rooms for the older children have helped her to feel grown-up. She remains a somewhat driven little girl — often competent, sometimes wryly humorous about herself, but going at things with an almost desperate intensity. I think that will ease, now that things in her home are a little more decided. And she's taught us a lot about how to work with her.

She comes in, says hello, scrambles up the ladder to the cat-walk into that sanctum sanctorum. Marcia has bustled in with a big smile and immediately bustled out again into the meadow. Janie is at the art table — another scarab? Danny's working with the letters for a change, Adam squatting beside him. Irene and Melissa are having their usual morning chat. I go over to them, and find myself using a phrase from my first months of internship: "Would you girls like to choose some work?"

The day's begun.